WALKS THROUGH

Napoleon & Josephine's

Paris

DIANA REID HAIG

The Little Bookroom ✦ New York

© 2004 by Diana Reid Haig
Design: Louise Fili & Chad Roberts, Louise Fili Ltd; Maps: Todd Pasini
Cover: Jacques-Louis David: Coronation of Emperor Napoleon I and Empress Josephine,
© RMN / Art Resource, New York.

Manufactured in China by South China Printing Company Ltd.
First Printing February 2004
10 9 8 7 6 5 4 3 2 1

Library of Congress Cataloging-in-Publication Data
Haig, Diana Reid
Walks through Napoleon and Josephine's Paris / by Diana Reid Haig.
   p. cm.
Includes bibliographical references and index.
ISBN 1-892145-25-1
1. Paris (France)--Description and travel. 2. Walking--France--Paris--Tours. 3. Paris (France)--History--Revolution, 1789-1799.
4. Paris (France)--History--Consulate and First Empire, 1799-1815. 5. Napoleon I, Emperor of the French, 1769-1821.
6. Josephine, Empress, consort of Napoleon I, Emperor of the French, 1763-1814. I. Title.
DC707.H19 2004
944.05'092'2--dc21
2003007632

Published by The Little Bookroom
1755 Broadway, Fifth floor, New York NY 10019
(212) 293-1643 Fax (212) 333-5374
editorial@littlebookroom.com
www.littlebookroom.com

For Elliot

Jean-Auguste-Dominique Ingres:
NAPOLEON BONAPARTE AS FIRST CONSUL

Antoine-Jean Gros:
PORTRAIT OF THE EMPRESS JOSEPHINE

TABLE OF CONTENTS

continued on next page

HOW TO USE THIS BOOK

FOR THE MOST PART, WALKS IN THE BOOK HAVE BEEN LAID OUT IN CHRONOLOGICAL ORDER. IN SEVERAL INSTANCES WHERE ARRANGING THE WALKS CHRONOLOGICALLY would lead the walker back and forth between the Left Bank and the Right Bank, an alternative route has been provided for the convenience of the walker.

Stops on the walk are indicated on each map by ⊕. Shops and restaurants of interest are listed on p. 114, and are indicated on the maps by Ⓐ.

Note: Napoleon gallicized the original Corsican spelling of his name from Napoleone Buonaparte to Napoleon Bonaparte when he married Rose de Beauharnais. At the same time, he also changed Rose's name to Josephine. To avoid confusion, the spelling of Napoleon's name has been standardized throughout the text as Napoleon Bonaparte. Josephine is referred to as Rose until the point in time when her name was changed.

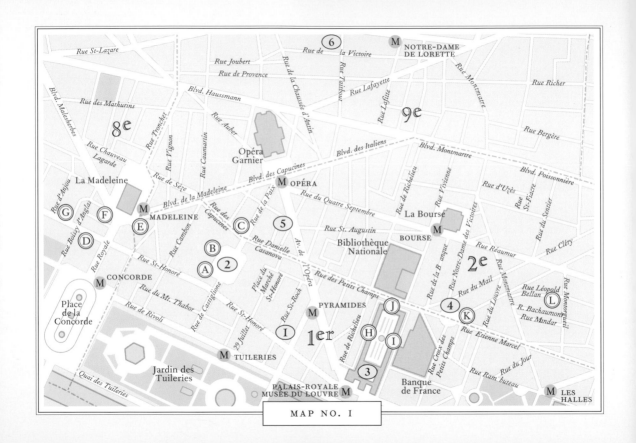

MAP NO. I

WALK 1

(M) METRO STOP

Jacques-Louis David:
GENERAL BONAPARTE

© RMN / Art Resource, New York

STOP 1 ✱ CHURCH OF SAINT-ROCH

296, RUE SAINT-HONORÉ
Métro: Pyramides

OCTOBER 5, 1795. RAIN POURED DOWN AS TWENTY-SIX-YEAR-OLD GENERAL NAPOLEON BONAPARTE FRANTICALLY SUPERVISED THE HAULING AND PLACEMENT OF FORTY cannons along the rue Saint-Honoré near the Church of Saint-Roch. His troops had been summoned to defend the Convention, France's ruling body, from almost 30,000 National Guard and Royalist rebels determined to gain control of Paris. Beating drums signaled an impending attack.

Six years had passed since the storming of the Bastille, and the government had changed hands numerous times. In September 1795, the Convention issued decrees preventing former Royalists from regaining power. Infuriated Royalists prepared to fight, and civil war seemed imminent. By October 3 the unrest in Paris had become a full-blown crisis, and General Paul Barras, Napoleon's former patron and head of the Army of the Interior, sent for him.

At that time Napoleon feared his military career was over. He had been suspended for refusing a transfer from the prestigious artillery to the infantry, and while he petitioned repeatedly for another artillery position he was working in a low-paying government job and living in a furnished room on the third floor of a cheap hotel by the Seine called the Blue Dial. Barras offered him command of all government artillery in Paris,

NAPOLEON'S TROOPS FIRE ON THE PARIS MOB ON THE STEPS OF THE CHURCH OF SAINT-ROCH.

Bibliothèque Nationale

provided that Napoleon accept the post within three minutes – Barras rightly suspected that Napoleon's resentment about his suspension might lead him to join the Royalists if they offered him a better deal. Napoleon agreed to take the position, and Barras immediately escorted him to the Tuileries palace where a special decree was written on the spot, reinstating Napoleon to his previous rank of general.

Hours later, Napoleon met the generals and troops under his command. They were outnumbered five to one, and their allegiance was uncertain. Despite these grave disadvantages, Napoleon believed that strategic positioning of cannons and continuous manning of artillery could win the battle. The Royalists decided to wait out the bad weather, then attacked just before 5pm with their best battalions. Napoleon rode up and down the narrow rue Saint-Honoré urging his men on. One general remembered that Napoleon, with his "frail appearance and dirty uniform, was everywhere at once." The combat extended as far as the Pont Neuf, which the Royalists had barricaded, but the most intense action was from the Théâtre de la République at the Palais-Royal to the steps of Saint-Roch, where Napoleon ruthlessly ordered his infamous "whiff of grapeshot" to be fired into the crowd. Napoleon's troops fought hard, inspired by his courage and electrifying presence. After his horse was shot from beneath him, he worked alongside the soldiers manning two huge cannons in a large open area facing Saint-Roch. Shots hit the church and the scars can still be seen faintly on the façade. Within an hour, the insurrection was suppressed, and more than a thousand Royalists lay dead in the streets. Luck had been with Napoleon; if the Royalists had attacked before the government artillery was in place, their superior numbers would have easily crushed his men.

Napoleon's bravery and brilliant use of artillery became the talk of the city, and he was promptly named Major General, commander in chief of the Army of the Interior, Governor of Paris, and head of the local police. He was given a large salary, headquarters in the Place Vendôme, a splendid coach with four horses, and spacious new lodging in rue des Capucines (see p.134). Paris had rarely seen a more unlikely hero. Small, pale, and unkempt, Napoleon was a loner who spoke with a heavy Italian accent-a far cry from the aristocratic French officers who were as comfortable in drawing rooms as on the battlefield. He was virtually unknown to Parisian society, lacked connections in the government, and was considered an insolent parvenu by the few at the Ministry of War who knew him.

Paul Barras continued to be Napoleon's mentor despite widespread skepticism that a Corsican should hold a high-ranking military position. He also profited from Napoleon's victory and quickly became the most important member of the new government, the Directory, which remained in power until 1799. Tall, charismatic, and decadent, the aristocratic Barras lived in style and had several mistresses. His current favorite was a charming thirty-one-year-old widowed ex-Vicomtesse whose husband had been guillotined during the last days of the Revolution. Her name was Rose de Beauharnais; within a year, she would be known as Napoleon's "Josephine."

Walk west on rue Saint-Honoré. Pass rue de la Sourdière and rue du Marché-Saint-Honoré. Turn right onto rue de Castiglione and walk to Place Vendôme.

STOP 2 ❋ PLACE VENDÔME

Métro: Tuileries

As the new head of the army of the interior, Napoleon was given an impressive office in the Place Vendôme. The Place Vendôme looks very much the same today as when it was built just before 1700; then, as now, it was one of the most beautiful public spaces in Paris. Napoleon's headquarters was likely at No. 7, which housed the Department of War.

Nine days after the Royalist insurrection, citizens living in Royalist sections of Paris were ordered to turn in all weapons; bayonets, swords, and axes were confiscated in a house-to-house search. Among the homes visited was one rented by Rose de Beauharnais, who lived there with her two children. Her husband, Vicomte Alexandre de Beauharnais, had been guillotined for crimes against the French. Beauharnais's sword was seized, despite the fact that Rose's thirteen-year-old son, Eugène, begged to keep it. Told that he could appeal to the commander in chief, Eugène presented himself at the Place Vendôme that afternoon. Napoleon later recounted:

Affected by the nature of Eugène's petition, I granted his request. Eugène burst into tears when he beheld his father's sword. Touched at his sensibility, I behaved so kindly to him that Madame de Beauharnais thought herself obligated to call on me the next day, to thank me for my attentions. Everyone knows (her) extraordinary grace...her irresistibly sweet, attractive manners. The acquaintance soon became intimate

Pierre-Paul Prud'hon:
PORTRAIT OF EMPRESS JOSEPHINE

RMN / Art Resource, New York

and tender. ...I was not insensible to women's charms, but I was shy with them. (She) was the first to give me confidence.

Like Napoleon, Rose had come to France from an island; an arranged marriage had brought her from her native Martinique. She was six years older than Napoleon but still looked very young. She was petite and spoke in a soft Creole drawl and, although her features were not classically beautiful, "She had a certain something which was irresistible," Napoleon later said. "She was a woman to her very fingertips." In a letter to her in December 1795, Napoleon wrote:

I awake all filled with you. Your image, and the intoxicating pleasures of last night, allow my senses no rest. ...A thousand kisses, mio dolce amor: *but give me none back, for they set my blood on fire.*

Not the least of Rose's appeal to Napoleon was that she was an insider in Parisian society. She was a member of the former aristocracy and had spent the year since her husband's death as confidante and hostess to important political figures including Paul Barras. Although Napoleon had settled effortlessly into his new administrative position, his sudden social advancement was more difficult. He was uncomfortable hosting luncheons and attending receptions and the opera, but with a former Vicomtesse by his side, his awkwardness was less obvious. He was determined to marry her.

Place Vendôme

The Vendôme Column, which stands at the center of the Place Vendôme, was plated with the bronze of 1,250 cannons captured from Austrian and Russian troops during the Battle of Austerlitz in 1805. It was modeled after Trajan's Column in Rome and features a spiral relief detailing scenes from camp life during this campaign and combat during the battle of Austerlitz, considered one of Napoleon's most brilliant victories.

Rue de Castiglione, on the south side of the Square, was built by Napoleon in 1802 to create a direct route from the Tuileries palace, where he was living, to Place Vendôme. He named it for his victory over the Austrians during the Italian campaign of 1796. In 1806 Napoleon also commissioned the building of a grand street from the north side of Place Vendôme. Originally called rue Napoléon, it is now named rue de la Paix. Today only one street in Paris-rue Bonaparte on the Left Bank-is named after Napoleon.

Early in February of 1796, Rose de Beauharnais went to the office of her *notaire*, Jean Raguideau, at No. 2, Place Vendôme to ask his opinion of her proposed marriage. Napoleon accompanied her and waited in the outer room while she explained the situation. Raguideau, unaware that Napoleon was listening outside the door, argued against a match to "a young man with nothing but his cloak and his sword." Although Napoleon recognized the prudence of Raguideau's counsel, the *notaire's* words left a lasting sting. On the day he was crowned in 1804, the Emperor summoned Raguideau to the Tuileries and, in his coronation robes, turned to him and asked, "Well, Raguideau, do I not now have more to recommend me than my cloak and my sword?"

Leave Place Vendôme on rue de la Paix, then turn right onto rue Danielle-Casanova. At avenue de l'Opéra, turn right and walk to place André-Malraux. At the fountains bear left. Enter the Palais-Royal through the arcades on the far side of the Comédie Française.

JARDIN DU PALAIS-ROYAL

Collection of the Author

STOP 3 ❖ PALAIS‑ROYAL

Métro: Palais-Royal/Musée du Louvre

Napoleon Bonaparte was in the Military School of Paris. My uncle Demetrius had met him just after he alighted from the coach which brought him to town. "And truly," said my uncle, "he had the appearance of a fresh importation. I met him in the Palais-Royal, where he was gaping and staring at everything he saw. He would have been an excellent subject for sharpers, if, indeed, he had had anything worth taking." - DUCHESSE D'ABRANTÈS

In 1780 THE DUC D'ORLÉANS, LOUIS XVI'S COUSIN, GAVE THE PALAIS AND ITS SURROUND-ING GARDENS AND THEATRES TO HIS HEDONISTIC SON, THE DUC DE CHARTRES, LATER known as Philippe Égalité. Perpetually short of cash, the duc de Chartres commissioned three arcades containing sixty apartments to be built around the gardens, named the surrounding streets after his three sons (Valois, Montpensier, and Beaujolais), then promptly rented the apartments as cafés, gambling houses, brothels, and boutiques. As property belonging to cousins of the king, the Palais-Royal was not subject to police raids, and it quickly became an infamous center of decadence that drew all classes of people. Eighteen-year-old Napoleon lost his virginity to a streetwalker that he met there in 1787.

If prostitution was the main business at the Palais-Royal, gambling was not far behind. Dozens of cafés featured magicians, ventriloquists, and novelty acts. The arcades also housed almost twenty of the city's finest restaurants, among them the Grand Véfour, where Napoleon and Josephine dined. The interiors of these restaurants were richly decorated and mirrors were often used to create illusions-a couple having dinner might see a thousand sparkling images of themselves reflected around the candlelit room. One of the most celebrated featured private dining areas with burning incense and sumptuous Oriental fabrics. On a signal, the ceiling of the dimly lit room would slide back and beautiful, barely clad young girls dressed as nymphs or pagan goddesses would descend from the ceiling on swings. Coffeehouses attracted intellectuals, lawyers, writers, and freethinkers. In the late 1780s, the Palais-Royal was one of the few places where pro-Revolutionary sentiments were openly discussed; here, in July of 1789, militant agitators incited a mob to storm the Bastille. The Palais-Royal became known as the "Birthplace of the Revolution," an ironic moniker for a property belonging to the king's relations. Just after 1800, the palace itself became home to the Tribunate, a branch of the French legislature.

After the Revolution, the Palais-Royal and the neighboring area continued to be the most stylish part of town and was filled with well-known merchants and luxury dressmakers. Rose was among their patrons, and for decades Napoleon bought his hats at 32, Galerie Montpensier (see p.106).

Leave the Palais-Royal by the north exit next to the Grand Véfour. Turn right onto rue de Beaujolais, left onto rue Vivienne, then take an immediate right onto rue des Petits-Champs. Continue straight on rue des Petits-Champs until it becomes rue la Feuillade, which leads to place des Victoires. Rue du Mail is on the north side of Place des Victoires.

STOP 4 ❊ SITE OF 12, RUE DU MAIL

Métro: Bourse

Duration THE BEGINNING OF THE REVOLUTION IN OCTOBER OF 1789, A CROWD MARCHED TO VERSAILLES AND FORCED LOUIS XVI AND MARIE ANTOINETTE TO PARIS, OSTENSIBLY to be near the people. They became unofficial prisoners in the Tuileries palace (destroyed in 1882) and were protected by loyal Swiss guards. In August 1792 revolutionary forces attacked the palace and slaughtered the guards. Napoleon, then a penniless 22-year-old army captain, was lodging nearby at the Hotel Metz. This boarding house, torn down in the 1790s, sat approximately where No. 12 rue du Mail is located today. Napoleon, who shared a small room on an upper floor with a former classmate from the military school at Brienne, later recalled:

> *I found myself lodging at the Mail in the Place des Victoires. …On learning that the Tuileries were under attack, I ran to the Carrousel. …Before reaching the Carrousel I had been met in the rue des Petits-Champs by a group of hideous men bearing a head at the end of a pike. Seeing that I was presentably dressed and had the appearance of a gentleman, they approached me and asked me to shout 'Long Live the Republic!' which you can easily imagine I did without difficulty.*

The Republican Calendar

To symbolize that a new era had begun with the ending of the monarchy, the Convention abolished the Gregorian calendar and introduced a new calendar, which began on the first day of the republic, September 22, 1792. The year still had twelve months, but each month was divided into three sections called decades, each lasting ten days. The months were named after seasons or events in nature: Vendemiaire (vintage; September-October), Brumaire (fog; October-November), Frimaire (frost; November-December), Nivose (snow; December-January), Pluviose (rain; January-February), Ventose (wind; February-March), Germinal (germination; March-April), Floreal (flower; April-May), Prairial (meadow; May-June), Messidor (harvest; June-July), Thermidor (warmth; July-August), Fructidor (fruit; August-September). Under the new system, all religious holidays, including Sundays, were abolished. The populace was allowed only one day of rest every tenth day. Because France was the only country using this notation, translating the dates for diplomatic matters and even simple correspondence became tiresome. Napoleon issued a decree discontinuing the Republican calendar on September 9, 1805.

Napoleon followed the crowd and arrived at the palace just after the killing had ended. What he saw turned his stomach:

The sight of the dead Swiss Guards gave me an idea of the meaning of death such as I have never had since, on any of my battlefields. … Perhaps it was because this was the first time I had undergone such an experience. I saw well-dressed women committing acts of the grossest indecency on the corpses… How far I was, as I watched the sack of the Tuileries, from imagining that I would ever live in that palace.

From the Place des Victoires, return along rue la Feuillade, which turns into rue des Petits-Champs, and then rue Danielle-Casanova. Turn right onto rue d'Antin.

STOP 5 ✳ 3, RUE D'ANTIN

Métro: Opéra

ON MARCH 9, 1796, NAPOLEON AND ROSE WERE MARRIED IN A DRAWING ROOM ON THE SECOND FLOOR OF THIS OLD MANSION, AT THAT TIME THE OFFICE OF THE MAIRIE OF the second arrondissement. They had known each other for little more than four months. Rose, dressed in a plain white gown with a patriotic tri-color sash, arrived for the civil ceremony just after 7pm with her notary and several witnesses. Around her neck she wore her wedding gift from Napoleon: a gold and enamel medallion with the simple inscription *Au destin* (To destiny).

Whenever Rose spoke of that night, she recalled watching the single candle in the room burn down to nothing in its tin holder while hours passed with no word from Napoleon. The official who was to perform the ceremony grew tired of waiting and left. Finally at 10pm, Napoleon bounded into the room with an aide-de-camp and exclaimed, "Marry us quickly!" Rose was never certain why he was so late, although there were rumors that he had been in his office falsifying his birth records. Both Rose and Napoleon lied about their ages and claimed to be 28; she took four years off hers, while he added eighteen months to his. A brief exchange of vows was performed by a low-ranking official who was later discovered to lack the proper legal authority. Although religious weddings had been outlawed during the Revolution, they could still be obtained quietly. Ironically, Rose preferred a civil ceremony, which would make it much easier to get a divorce. She still harbored doubts about marrying a man without savings or property.

Neither Rose's nor Napoleon's families attended the wedding, but one witness was Paul Barras, head of the Directory. Though Rose had recently been his mistress, Barras, weary of Rose's extravagance, encouraged her to marry Napoleon. Napoleon later said, "Barras did me a good turn when he advised me to marry Josephine. He pointed out that she was a member of both the old regime and the new, that the marriage would make people forget my Corsican name, would make me wholly French."

There was no time for a prolonged honeymoon. Napoleon was leaving in two days to take command of the Army of Italy, a promotion rumored to be a wedding present from Barras. Before his departure, Napoleon decided his name should be gallicized from the original Corsican spelling, Napoleone Buonaparte, to Napoleon Bonaparte, and he renamed his new wife Josephine, derived from her maiden name Marie-Josephe-Rose Tascher de la Pagerie.

Walk north on avenue de l'Opéra to the Opéra métro. Take the No. 8 Métro line (toward Balard) to the Madeleine. Change to the No. 12 (toward Porte de la Chapelle) to Notre-Dame-de-Lorette.

STOP 6 ❋ SITE OF 60, RUE DE LA VICTOIRE

ORIGINALLY 6, RUE CHANTEREINE

Métro: Notre-Dame-de-Lorette

IN THE FALL OF 1795, THE WIDOWED VICOMTESSE ROSE DE BEAUHARNAIS MOVED INTO AN ELEGANT LITTLE HOUSE AT NO. 6, RUE CHANTEREINE. ALTHOUGH SHE WAS COMPENSATED for her first husband's property, seized before his execution, Rose was living beyond her means, had no permanent way to support herself or her two children, Eugène and Hortense, and was deeply in debt. Her only hope was an alliance with a rich, powerful man, but to accomplish this, she felt it was important to give the impression that she was a woman of independent wealth. She approached a banker and asked to borrow against future earnings from her share of her family's sugar plantation in Martinique.

Her loan granted, Rose bought beautiful clothes, decorated her home, sent her children to boarding school, and began to look for a wealthy protector. She had been imprisoned during the Revolution, and prison life had taken a toll on her. At thirty-two, her health was often poor; her teeth had been neglected and now were practically black stubs. To disguise this problem, she perfected the art of a tight-lipped smile and used her eyes to express her feelings. She furnished her home simply but exquisitely. Determined to create the illusion that she was wealthy, Rose hired eight servants and filled the house with flowers to hide the fact that she had few paintings and little furniture. She spent lavishly on fine food and wine for her guests, yet had to borrow household necessities such as pots and pans. Most significantly, she quickly assembled a salon, inviting painters, actors, beautiful women, influential men of the new Republican government, and noble families she had known since her first marriage.

Later, after she and Napoleon married, they lived together at No. 6, rue Chantereine. As Napoleon's successes on the battlefield multiplied, the house began to attract sightseers, and Parisians began calling Josephine "Our Lady of Victories." In 1797 a grateful municipal council changed the name of the street where the couple lived to rue de la Victoire. Hortense recalled:

> *General Bonaparte arrived from Italy. Paris rang with his name. Everyone sought to catch a glimpse of him in order to admire him. He lived at my mother's house in the rue Chantereine, which was promptly rechristened rue de la Victoire. …What a change had come over our little home that formerly was so quiet. Now it was filled with generals and officers. The sentinels had difficulty in keeping back a crowd made up of all classes of people, impatient and eager to catch sight of the conqueror of Italy.*

Immediately after her marriage, Josephine began a passionate three-year affair with Hippolyte Charles, a young lieutenant whom she met after Napoleon left for Italy. Josephine and Charles were also involved financially; they secretly went into business together to sell substandard army supplies to Napoleon's troops at substantial mark-ups. At first the couple met surreptitiously at the house on rue Chantereine. Later, Josephine recklessly allowed herself to be seen with him in public, even allowing him to travel with her to Italy to visit Napoleon. One of the passengers in the coach on that trip was Napoleon's brother Joseph, who quickly detected his sister-in-law's infidelity and told Napoleon and the rest of the family.

When Napoleon first heard rumors of Josephine's affair, he confronted her. She tearfully denied everything and continued to see Charles. Napoleon learned conclusively of her adultery when he was in Egypt in 1799 and wrote to his brother that he was determined to divorce her. A British warship captured the French boat carrying the mailbag and the English press gleefully printed Napoleon's letter in the newspapers. Upon hearing that Napoleon had returned to France, Josephine hurried to meet him en route, determined to present her side of the story before Napoleon's brothers could reach him. Napoleon traveled by an alternate road and arrived to an empty house. Enraged, he assumed that Josephine had left him for Charles, a belief encouraged by the Bonaparte clan, who had always loathed Josephine.

Napoleon ordered all of Josephine's belongings removed and, when she finally arrived back in Paris three days later, she found that the guard had been given orders not to let her in. In tears, she pushed by and ran into the house to find that Napoleon had locked himself in an upstairs room. After hours of hysterical pleading, Josephine crouched exhausted outside the door at the top of the narrow winding stairs. Not until dawn, when Josephine's children begged him to see her, did the door open. Napoleon would forgive Josephine but no longer trust her, although there was never another rumor about her having an affair. Over the next few years, Josephine fell in love with her husband, but Napoleon, who had started to take mistresses while in Egypt, continued his

Eric Pape:
JOSEPHINE AT THE DOOR OF
BONAPARTE'S CHAMBER

New York Public Library Picture Collection

affairs, often flaunting them in his wife's face.

Only a few weeks after the couple's reconciliation, the famous coup d'état of 18 Brumaire (November 9, 1799) was planned at No. 60, rue de la Victoire by high-level political figures who sought to use Napoleon, newly returned from Egypt, as a figurehead to gain control of the government from the corrupt Directory. Since Napoleon did not have an office at that time, he used rue de la Victoire as his base. Night and day couriers galloped down the path leading to the house with urgent messages for the General. As the coup drew nearer, Josephine used all her connections to help her husband. She entertained government officials, hoping that these occasions would give them the opportunity to see Napoleon in a more flattering light. In addition, Josephine's regular evening receptions allowed the conspirators a chance to meet discreetly.

During two dramatic days in early November, Napoleon took control of the government. After the coup, Napoleon arrived back at rue de la Victoire around 3am with his secretary, Bourrienne, who remembered that when Napoleon said goodnight, he added "by the way, tomorrow we sleep at the Luxembourg Palace." That night was the last time that Napoleon and Josephine spent the night in a house as private citizens.

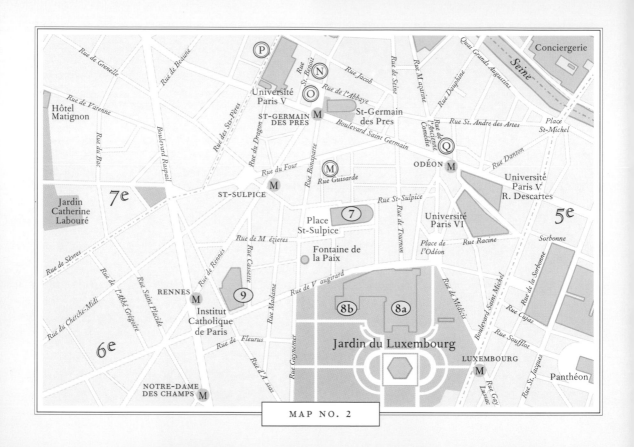

MAP NO. 2

WALK 2

(M) METRO STOP

François Gérard:
PORTRAIT OF BONAPARTE

STOP 7 ❋ CHURCH OF SAINT-SULPICE

THREE DAYS BEFORE THE COUP D'ÉTAT OF 18 BRUMAIRE (NOVEMBER 9, 1799), IMPORTANT GOVERNMENT OFFICIALS DROVE THROUGH A HAILSTORM TO ATTEND A GRAND BANQUET at the Church of Saint-Sulpice, then called the Temple of Victory. Although the event was ostensibly to honor Napoleon and another general, all eyes were on Napoleon, who was rumored to be conspiring to overthrow the Directory. The dinner quickly turned into a farce. Guests sat shivering in the drafty church, and gossip about the possibility of an impending coup—plotted by the guest of honor against his hosts—could not be quieted. Some even took bets as to whether the next few days would take Napoleon to the Luxembourg or the guillotine. When the general arrived, he sat in silence, glowering at the dignitaries who toasted him, making no secret of his suspicion that he might be poisoned. After refusing everything offered him from the lavish dinner, guests watched in silence as Napoleon carefully unpacked his own meager supper of a pear, a few slices of bread, and wine.

✦

During the Revolution, churches were closed or used as prisons, assembly halls, or for storage. Saint-Sulpice served as a warehouse for grains and hay, and each of the church's towers was converted into a semaphore sta-

SAINT-SULPICE

Private collection

tion to relay military and political information. The semaphore, a crude version of the telegraph, used lights and flags to send messages and information and it could only be operated in clear weather. The south tower communicated with Orléans and Bordeaux, while the north tower was linked to Lyon. Each station needed at least two men, one to receive messages while peering into a telescope and another to relay messages. Although many churches were destroyed during the Revolution, the height of Saint-Sulpice's twin towers, necessary for the semaphore system to run smoothly, ensured the building's safety.

With your back to the church, turn left and walk south on rue Bonaparte. Cross rue de Mézières and pass the Fontaine de la Paix, commissioned by Napoleon in 1806, near 92, rue Bonaparte. Turn right onto rue de Vaugirard then a quick left onto rue Guynemer. Turn left into le Jardin du Luxembourg (Luxembourg Gardens) and pass l'Orangerie. The Petit Luxembourg is on your left behind high foliage and a fence. Walk to the end of the fence for a better view.

François Bouchot:
THE EIGHTEENTH OF BRUMAIRE

© RMN / Art Resource, NY

STOP 8 ✦ LUXEMBOURG PALACE & PETIT LUXEMBOURG

15 & 17, RUE DE VAUGIRARD
Métro: Notre-Dame-des-Champs

To the People

19th Brumaire, 11 o'clock, pm

Citizens! I found discord pervading every department of the government. The authorities agreed only on this single truth: that the constitution was half-destroyed and unable to protect our liberty.

So WROTE NAPOLEON IN A DRAMATIC PROCLAMATION EXPLAINING HIS COUP D'ÉTAT OF 18-19 BRUMAIRE (NOV. 9-10, 1799), WHICH ELIMINATED THE DIRECTORY, INTRODUCED the Consulate, and quickly made him the most powerful man in France.

The morning after he seized control of the government, Napoleon, along with Josephine, Hortense, Eugène, and their servants arrived at the Luxembourg. Promptly renamed the Palais du Consulate, it housed the living quarters and offices of the other two consuls, who had already been residing there as members of the Directory. The palace had not been refurbished since its tenure as a jail in the early 1790s and was in a state of disrepair. Predictably, Barras's former rooms were the most lavish, but Napoleon disapproved of the decadence of the last regime and selected fairly modest quarters located to the west of the main palace in the Petit Luxembourg.

The three-story Petit Luxembourg is a quaint, shuttered hôtel adjacent to the western wing of the main palace; it is visible only through the gardens. Napoleon's personal suite was on the ground floor. A stairway led to Josephine's rooms, one flight up. Napoleon enjoyed living there because it enabled him to return to work at any hour, and he was always happy to be closeted in his small, plain office. When in Paris Napoleon's days followed a fairly predictable schedule. He had a simple breakfast of roasted chicken promptly at ten o'clock with Josephine and Hortense. The rest of the day was spent in meetings and reviewing correspondence. At five o'clock dinner was served and, as Napoleon ate very quickly, sometimes the entire meal would not last more than fifteen minutes. Afterwards, Napoleon would visit his wife in her apartments. The First Consul usually spent the evening in conference with his ministers while Josephine entertained their guests. At midnight, Napoleon, wearing his white dressing gown with a madras handkerchief on his head, would relax with Josephine and then return to work. Pacing back and forth across the carpet, hands wrapped around a cup of hot chocolate, he dictated letters and orders to his exhausted secretary, Bourrienne, who often fell asleep at his desk. At 3 or 4am, Napoleon ordered sherbet or ice cream, took a hot bath, and after several hours sleep, began his day again.

As wife of the most powerful man in the new government, Josephine's life changed dramatically. At Napoleon's request, she presided over many charities and became his intermediary with members of the former aristocracy who wanted to return to France. Napoleon had forbidden Josephine to see most of her old friends because of their scandalous reputations and she often felt isolated. Though she would occasionally sneak out to the theatre, for the most part, Josephine obeyed her husband's orders. Napoleon's network of spies kept him abreast of his wife's movements, and she feared angering him. To console herself, she redecorated her rooms and spent wildly on gowns and jewelry.

Napoleon's first priority during the Consulate was to restore domestic order and financial stability. Seemingly overnight, he blossomed into an astute financier and a talented politician with prodigious administrative skills. He created the *Banque de France*, solved chronic bread shortages, reformed education, introduced a system for renumbering many streets in Paris, and ordered the creation of a new Civil Code so that the entire country would soon operate under one set of laws. He also proposed a new Constitution that gave him principal decision-making authority. On February 7, 1800, more than three million Frenchmen—an overwhelming majority—voted for Napoleon to become First Consul, the ancient title bestowed upon Junius Brutus, First Consul of the Roman Republic. As soon as the vote was in, Napoleon began planning to move to a more imposing palace, the Tuileries, adjacent to the Louvre and last inhabited by Louis XVI and Marie Antoinette.

On the afternoon of February 19, 1800, Napoleon left the Luxembourg Palace in an ostentatious procession headed for the Tuileries. Led by 3,000 soldiers in colorful new uniforms, the consuls rode together from the Luxembourg in a carriage drawn by six white horses. That day, the three men shared the applause, but Napoleon would soon have the spotlight to himself.

✦

During the early 1790s, when the Luxembourg was used as a prison, its inmates included Alexandre de

Jacques-Louis David: VIEW OF THE GARDEN OF THE LUXEMBOURG IN PARIS

Beauharnais, Josephine's first husband, who was briefly held there in 1794 before being moved to the Carmes prison. The artist and revolutionary Jacques-Louis David, later named First Painter to Napoleon, was also imprisoned there that year. David, who went on to create many famous portraits of Napoleon, including *Coronation of Emperor Napoleon I and Empress Josephine*, painted his only landscape, the view from his prison window, while under arrest at the Luxembourg (see facing page). The painting gives an idea of what the gardens surrounding the Luxembourg looked like during the Revolution. The houses on rue de Vaugirard can also be seen; the Carmes prison, where Josephine was held, is located just beyond.

During the Empire, the Senate met at the Luxembourg. Today the palace is still home to the French Senate.

> *Facing the palace from the garden, walk around the right side of the Luxembourg and turn left onto rue de Vaugirard. Continue straight on rue de Vaugirard past rue Bonaparte and rue Madame to Saint-Joseph-des-Carmes, just before the Institut Catholique at the intersection of rue de Vaugirard and rue d'Assas.*

STOP 9 ✦ SAINT‑JOSEPH‑DES‑CARMES

70, RUE DE VAUGIRARD
Métro: Rennes

Tours of the crypt, jail, and gardens are usually given on Saturday at 3pm. For entrance at other times, inquire inside the church at the sacristy to the left of the altar. The church is usually open during the day, except during late July and the entire month of August.

UPON ENTERING THE CHURCH OF SAINT‑JOSEPH‑DES‑CARMES THERE IS A SMALL DOOR JUST TO THE LEFT OF THE HIGH ALTAR MARKED "SACRISTIE DES MESSES." BEHIND THIS unremarkable entry lies one of the most ominous sites in Paris: the prison of the Carmes where Rose de Beauharnais was jailed in 1794. A long series of steps leads down to the cells, which are partially intact today. This prison, considered among the worst in Paris, had a gruesome history. On a Sunday afternoon in September 1792, a Revolutionary crowd stormed through the Left Bank and forced their way into the Carmes. They held mock trials for the prisoners, most of whom had been arrested for being priests or aristocrats, before killing them. Many of the priests tried to escape and were bludgeoned to death at the bottom of the stairs leading into the garden behind the church. The dead included 115 priests and three bishops, all of whom were later beatified. This grim episode and similar ones at other prisons became known as the September Massacres. The bones

Coiffure à la Guillotine

In contrast to the elaborate powdered coiffures popularized by Marie Antoinette, the hairstyles of the 1790s reflected the turmoil of the Revolution, when all prisoners facing death had their hair shorn before they were guillotined. While a prisoner at the Carmes, Rose cut her hair to save herself the indignity of being shorn by the executioner's assistant. After her release from prison, Rose kept her hair short as a reminder of what she had endured. This style, appropriately called coiffure à la guillotine, became popular, and soon many women were wearing their hair cropped.

of these martyrs, found in a well outside the Carmes, are displayed today in glass cases in the church's crypt.

The Reign of Terror, the most violent phase of the French Revolution, began in 1793 and peaked during June and July of 1794, while Rose was imprisoned. She had been arrested on April 22, 1794 on the basis of an anonymous letter sent to the Committee of Public Safety that read, "Beware of the former vicomtesse, wife of Alexandre Beauharnais, who has many secret connections with the government." Deputies led her away late at night. Hortense later wrote: *"What intense grief we felt when we were told she had entered our room to bid us farewell. …She had not wished our slumber to be disturbed. 'Let them sleep,' she said to our governess, 'I could not bear the sight of their sorrow. I would not have the strength to part from them.'"*

In the 1790s, entry to the prison was through the large walled back garden, which exists today but cannot be seen from rue de Vaugirard. Prisoners were led in and out near the spot where the priests had been murdered. The prison was almost entirely underground, and seven hundred prisoners were crammed into damp stone cells overrun by rats. They were fed pickled herring, which they had to buy, and were allowed one bottle of water a day for all purposes. There were no latrines and the stench was overpowering. Male prisoners were usually isolated from female prisoners, although they were allowed to meet for meals and sometimes at night. If it was discovered that a female inmate was pregnant, her trial was postponed until after she had given birth. This, combined with the desperate loneliness of prison life, led to extreme sexual permissiveness. Sounds of erotic couplings were commonplace in the halls late at night.

One celebrated prisoner of the Carmes was Grace Elliott, a blonde English aristocrat who had been the lover of the duc d'Orléans, Louis XVI's cousin and was now one of Rose's cellmates. Elliott wrote,

I met Madame Beauharnais the night of my arrival. Before we went to bed, we were as good friends as if we had been brought up together. Indeed, we expected every day might be our last. We were in fear of the mob breaking into the prison and renewing the scenes of (the) September (massacre)—scenes we could not forget, for the walls and even the wooden chairs were still stained with the blood and brains of the priests. Most of the prisoners, like myself, had little reason to hope they would leave the walls of the Carmes, but for the scaffold; yet, in spite of this horrid prospect, I must own that I passed many pleasant moments with these agreeable women, all full of talent, none more so than Madame Beauharnais. She is one of the most good-humoured women I ever met. We often washed the room together, for the other prisoners did not take much pains about it.

Prisoners were not permitted to correspond with their families. Bundles of clean linen and food were allowed to be sent to each inmate, however, and Rose's children took turns writing out the list of each package's contents, hoping that their parents would see their handwriting and know that they were still alive. Eugène and Hortense also used Rose's small dog, Fortuné, as a messenger, writing notes and hiding them under his collar. The dog would dash through the legs of the guards and find his mistress inside, often returning with a hastily scribbled note from Rose, whose health was failing rapidly as a result of prison conditions.

On July 22, 1794, Vicomte Beauharnais was guillotined. Rose learned of her husband's death several days later when she saw his name on a list of the executed. Knowing that widows were usually called to trial immediately following their husbands, Rose fainted, and a prison doctor was brought to examine her. His prognosis—that Rose was too ill to survive more than a few days—inadvertently saved her life. Rose was left in her cell. A day or two later, Robespierre was executed, ending the Reign of Terror. Rose was among the first to be released.

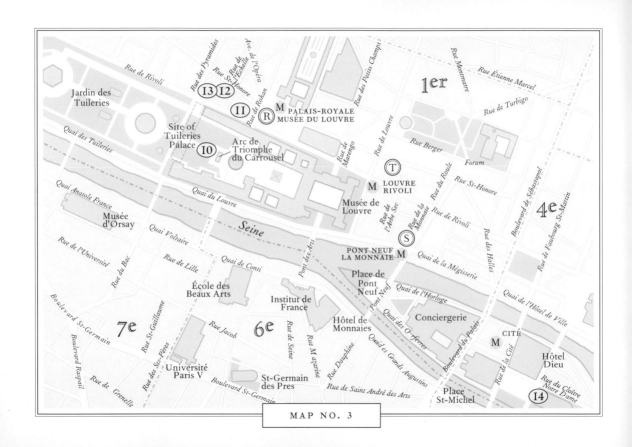

MAP NO. 3

WALK 3

Bellangé: MILITARY REVIEW AT THE TUILERIES

Bellangé-Dauzats

STOP 10 ✸ SITE OF THE TUILERIES PALACE

THE TUILERIES SAT BETWEEN THE ARC DE TRIOMPHE DU CARROUSEL AND THE TUILERIES GARDEN
Métro: Palais-Royal/Musée du Louvre

This walk follows the route of Napoleon and Josephine as they traveled by coach from the Tuileries to Notre-Dame for their Coronation on December 2, 1804. The parade began at the Carrousel of the Tuileries palace (where the Arc de Triomphe du Carrousel, commissioned by Napoleon in 1806, stands today), traveled up rue Saint-Honoré, and crossed the Seine at the Pont Neuf before ending at Notre-Dame. Several streets around the Louvre used by the parade were demolished during the late 1800s. Rue de Rivoli, slightly to the west, will be substituted instead, and the original route will resume a few blocks later on rue Saint-Honoré. The Tuileries was burned by rioters in 1871 and demolished in 1882.

THE TUILERIES SERVED AS NAPOLEON'S PRIMARY OFFICIAL RESIDENCE FOR ALMOST FOURTEEN YEARS. HE MOVED IN ON FEBRUARY 19, 1800. WHEN HIS CARRIAGE ROLLED to a stop, he stepped out and immediately mounted a white horse to begin the first of many legendary military reviews he conducted in the rectangular cobblestoned courtyard in front of the palace. While Josephine and Hortense watched from an upper window, an officer shouted "*le Premier consul*," and Napoleon began a quick gallop through the ranks followed by an inspection of each battalion as they marched by.

Fashion

The fashions worn at the court of Marie Antoinette included large panniers, the hoops used to extend skirts to the right and left. Following the Revolution, Josephine dressed in a more simple style, wearing plain, fitted gowns of white muslin or tulle so diaphanous as to be practically transparent. The dresses, which featured deep décolletage and a high waist, are still known as the Empire Style. Dresses made during the Directory, Consulate, and Empire years usually had no pockets, which led to the invention of a dainty bag called a réticule, made from net or fabric, which held handkerchiefs, sewing items, or other objects. As Empress, Josephine owned more than sixty rare and costly cashmere shawls and almost five hundred wraps and large scarves. Slippers, jewelry, and ornate fans, inlaid with gold and silver, finished a well-dressed Parisian woman's ensemble. Before her marriage to Napoleon, Josephine was part of an extreme fashion group called the Merveilleuses who frequented the Palais-Royal wearing bodystockings, gold ornamental bands around their legs, and even wigs tinted pale blue, blond, or light pink. Napoleon's interest in fashion was primarily fiscal. Eager to invigorate the economy, he encouraged the revival of luxury goods, which had all but vanished during the early years of the Revolution. Instead of cotton and muslin, silk manufactured in Lyon began to be used. Napoleon was furious if he found any member of his family wearing dresses made from British fabric, even going so far as to tear offending garments in two.

The Arc de Triomphe du Carrousel—the main entrance to the courtyard where these reviews were held—and the gardens that sat behind the palace are almost all that remain of the Tuileries. In medieval times, factories for making tiles (*tuiles*) were located in the area where the palace was built in the mid-1500s by Catherine de Médicis. The palace had been used during the Revolution as government offices; in mid-1795 Napoleon worked there in the topographical office of the Committee of Public Safety. Vendors had opened stalls selling pastry and tobacco, and a barber had set up shop. When Napoleon and Josephine moved in, the palace was filthy and run down. Josephine had been given the ground-floor apartments of Marie Antoinette and spent her first day at the new home in tears. "I can still recall my mother's melancholy…she kept imagining she saw poor Marie Antoinette everywhere," Hortense wrote. To Josephine's horror, her suite faced the gardens, which were open to the public, and crowds of people tried to peer in her windows.

Napoleon and Josephine soon opened the social season in Paris with dazzling official receptions at the Tuileries. Flickering candles and exotic flowers transformed the palace, and hundreds of women in jewels and feathers climbed the grand marble staircase and spilled out of Josephine's salons into the mirrored hallways. Napoleon and Josephine also began to host monthly banquets for a hundred guests in the Gallery of Diana, the spectacular state dining hall famous for its five enormous crystal chandeliers. The First Consul appeared at these events out of uniform, dressed in a crimson coat richly embroidered with gold, and wearing a magnificent new ceremonial sword with the 140-carat Regent diamond glittering from its hilt. The famous hairdresser Duplan wove flowers, pearls, and precious stones among Josephine's dark curls and she wore exquisite low-cut evening

Le Palais des Tuileries

Even after Napoleon ordered that his household move from one château to another, re-creating the "royal progresses" of the Bourbons and other kings, the Tuileries remained his headquarters. Napoleon spent more time at the Tuileries than at any other home: every winter and part of the summer. He ordered identical furniture for all his private rooms, although the upholstery differed from palace to palace, and had the pieces placed in the same positions in every château. Even the books in the library were shelved in the same order so they could be found quickly. Although the Tuileries no longer exists, Napoleon's private apartments at Fontainebleau and Versailles's Grand Trianon resemble his rooms there.

Josephine's suite in the Tuileries lay directly under Napoleon's, connected by a small spiral staircase. Napoleon would spend the night with his wife in her bedroom, then return the following morning to his own apartments to bathe, dress, and start work. These rooms, previously used by Louis XVI, included a heavily guarded map room used in planning military campaigns and Napoleon's private study, furnished with green morocco chairs, ebony tables, and an imposing mechanical desk (now at Malmaison) made of ormolu-mounted mahogany. Runners allowed the top of the desk to swing under the writing section so that it could be closed without disturbing papers. Two bookcases lined the walls, and between them stood a six-foot clock called a regulator. Napoleon's favorite settee, upholstered in green taffeta, was placed just to the left of the fireplace.

dresses of pale velvet or satin. Napoleon often helped select her gown—one of Josephine's ladies-in-waiting noted that when Napoleon appeared in his wife's dressing room "he caused complete chaos." With her husband's approval, Josephine hired a librarian to help her learn all the members of the various courts of Europe. She memorized foreign protocol, and guests came away impressed with her style and sophistication. Napoleon remarked, "I only win battles. Josephine wins hearts for me."

In March of 1802, Napoleon signed the treaty of Amiens with England and, for the first time in a decade, Europe was at peace. In August 1802 Napoleon was named Consul for life. Napoleon and Josephine had been unable to have children, and now Josephine became obsessed by the idea that her husband would divorce her for a younger woman who would be able to provide Napoleon with an heir. Angered by her jealousy, Napoleon began to sleep in his own bedroom and use a suite on the top floor for liaisons with other women.

In May of 1804, the French Senate, informed by Napoleon of his aspiration to be a monarch, cast a vote, ratified by the people, that the 34-year-old Consul would become "Napoleon, Emperor of the French." Napoleon threw himself into preparations for his Coronation with the same indefatigable energy he used to plan a battle. He mapped out the parade route, selected his coat-of-arms, endlessly discussed what should be worn, and ordered that Charlemagne's sword and crown be brought out for the ceremony. Napoleon asked Pope Pius VII to break from centuries of tradition and to crown him not at the cathedral at Rheims, but at Notre-Dame. Negotiations about this unprecedented matter went on so long that the festivities were rescheduled several times. After much deliberation, Napoleon chose a golden eagle holding a thunderbolt in its claws—a sym-

G.J. Vibert: La Répétition du Sacre

Collection of the author

bol reminiscent of ancient Rome—as his imperial insignia. The Emperor also selected a bee, a symbol of industry. Soon the eagle and the bee adorned robes, tapestries, rugs, dresses, cloaks, carriages, linens, and china. Even Josephine's slippers had golden bees embroidered on them.

Throughout the preparations, Napoleon remained undecided about whether Josephine should be crowned. Although the meddling Bonapartes escalated their efforts to convince their brother to divorce his wife before the Coronation, ultimately Napoleon chose to make her Empress, saying "she should share my success. ...Yes, she will be crowned." Several days before the ceremony, Napoleon ordered Josephine's favorite artist Jean-Baptiste Isabey to paint watercolors illustrating the main parts of the ceremony. Unable to do this in such a short time, Isabey bought hundreds of dolls, had them dressed in costumes identical to those being worn in the ceremony and set them up on a miniature stage set of Notre Dame so that Napoleon could envision the ceremony. The day before the Coronation, Josephine met privately with the Pope and confessed that she and Napoleon had been married in a civil ceremony, and were therefore unwed in the eyes of the Church. As she had anticipated, the stunned Pope demanded that a nuptial Mass immediately take place or he would not participate in the Coronation. Napoleon reluctantly agreed and that night the couple was quietly remarried before a makeshift altar in Napoleon's study at the Tuileries.

✦

A light snow fell the night before the Coronation. Although it was bitterly cold, thousands filled the streets, quays, and bridges to see the new Emperor and Empress in *le Cortège du Sacre*. All around the capital, festivities had begun. Houses and shops had been gaily decorated with brilliant tapestries and bright artificial flowers. Windows and roofs overlooking the parade route rented for astronomical prices. The population of Paris had nearly doubled during Coronation week as more than a million people arrived from the provinces and abroad.

At 8am the snow stopped, and a light fog rolled over the city as government dignitaries set out in carriages for Notre-Dame, escorted by hundreds of horsemen and foot-soldiers wearing red-plumed helmets. An hour later at the Tuileries, the elderly Pope, in a simple white robe, was helped into his golden coach. The Pope was preceded by an Italian chamberlain mounted on a mule and carrying a huge ornate cross on his back—the custom in Rome whenever the Pope traveled. Irreverent Parisians roared with laughter at the unexpected sight of a mule amidst such splendor, but grew still as the Pope came into view. They watched him with great interest, although few knelt to receive his benediction.

At the stroke of ten, bursts of artillery announced that Napoleon and Josephine were ready to depart from the Tuileries. The governor of Paris, trumpeters, and drummers headed the parade, followed by four squadrons of cavalry on prancing horses, and four of cuirassiers, mounted soldiers wearing armor and helmets. Regiments of Horse Chasseurs of the Guard followed and, finally, the exotic Mamelukes, Arab soldiers in turbans who had joined Napoleon's army in Egypt. Long lines of heralds, wearing lavender coats and carrying flags, stretched as far as the eye could see. Thirty gilded coaches carried the dignitaries. Napoleon had given orders for the parade to move as briskly as possible because his spies had warned of possible assassination attempts. However, as the huge coaches wheeled through the narrow streets, the procession slowed to a crawl, sometimes coming to a complete stop. Napoleon's aides rode up and down, watching the crowd carefully for signs of danger.

At last applause was heard as the gleaming Imperial coach appeared, topped with four silver eagles carrying a crown. All four sides were made of glass and the interior was lined with velvet. Inside sat Napoleon in a crimson velvet cloak, with Josephine beside him, diamonds shimmering from her hair to her waist.

Following the signs to the Pavillon de Rohan, walk north from the Place du Carrousel to the intersection of rue de Rivoli and rue de Rohan.

RUE DE RIVOLI

Collection of the author

STOP 11 ❉ RUE DE RIVOLI

FROM THE LOUVRE TO RUE DES PYRAMIDES
Métro: Palais-Royal/Musée du Louvre

WHILE NAPOLEON MADE MANY IMPORTANT URBAN IMPROVEMENTS TO PARIS, RUE DE RIVOLI, CREATED TO EASE THE HEAVY TRAFFIC ON RUE SAINT-HONORÉ ONE BLOCK north, is one of his best-loved contributions. He directed his favorite architects, Charles Percier and Pierre Fontaine, to construct the part of the street which runs from place de la Concorde to place du Palais-Royal. Percier and Fontaine planned the famous shopping arcades and designed the uniform façades of the buildings. The street, named for one of Napoleon's victories in the Italian campaign, runs through the site of the old Feuillants monastery, which had been named for the twenty thousand white mulberry trees planted here by Henri IV in 1600. Some of Napoleon's top generals are among the military statues that decorate the Louvre's façade along rue de Rivoli.

> *Continue on rue de Rivoli to place des Pyramides with its golden statue of Joan of Arc. Turn right onto rue des Pyramides. At rue Saint-Honoré, turn right and continue east.*

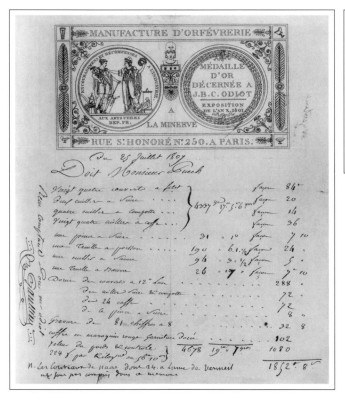

TRADE CARD OF MARTIN GUILLAUME BIENNAIS

The Metropolitan Museum of Art, Gift of Mrs. Bella C. Landauer

BILL OF JEAN BAPTISTE CLAUDE ODIOT

The Metropolitan Museum of Art, Gift of Mrs. Bella C. Landauer

STOP 12 ✷ RUE SAINT-HONORÉ

Métro: Palais-Royal/Musée du Louvre

ALTHOUGH LARGE COACHES COULD MANEUVER MORE EASILY ON WIDER THOROUGHFARES, IT WAS IMPOSSIBLE FOR THE CORONATION PARADE TO AVOID TRAVELING DOWN THE narrow rue Saint-Honoré, at that time the main east-west artery of the Right Bank. Known for its fashionable shops, the street also had darker associations—during the Revolution, it served as the route used by the tumbrils, open carts that transported almost 3,000 victims from prison to the guillotine set up in what is now the Place de la Concorde.

In his early years at the Tuileries, the First Consul often enjoyed slipping out of his office in the evening and strolling down rue Saint-Honoré with his secretary, Bourrienne, who later wrote of these excursions:

In his gray coat, Bonaparte would take my arm, and we would go to buy some article of trifling value in the shops of rue Saint-Honoré. ...Nothing was more amusing than seeing him imitate the young men of fashion. Putting on dandy airs while pulling up the corners of his cravat, he would say, "Well, Madame, is there anything new today? What do people say of that buffoon Bonaparte?"

Many purveyors patronized by the Emperor were located on rue Saint-Honoré, including Biennais, the goldsmith, and Odiot, the silversmith. Napoleon bought many swords and other items from Biennais, housed at No. 283, and famous for its sign of the Singe Violet (Purple Monkey) which hung outside. Biennais was commissioned by Napoleon to create a portable toiletry case that the young General took with him to Egypt. Odiot and Biennais later created most of the Coronation regalia, including Napoleon's crown of golden laurel leaves.

Café de la Régence, at No. 161, rue Saint-Honoré, was Napoleon's favorite place to play chess when he was a young officer. As early as 1777, the most skillful players in Paris would meet at this coffeehouse, headquarters for an unofficial chess club that included Benjamin Franklin. For years, the café displayed the table upon which Napoleon liked to play; the café closed in the early 1900s.

In the early years of her first marriage, Rose de Beauharnais shopped for gowns at Rose Bertin's boutique, which stood at No. 149, rue Saint-Honoré. According to one bill, her purchases included several expensive shawls, twenty-two yards of gray taffeta, and two pairs of gray stockings with colored geometric patterns. Bertin, an imaginative couturière, was the favorite dressmaker of Marie Antoinette.

Rue Saint-Honoré was unpaved during the early 1800s and when it rained or snowed, boards were put down so that pedestrians could cross the flooded street. Women, clutching their shawls and lifting the hems of their dresses to avoid the mud, would gingerly tiptoe over the planks or, for a fee, hire a man to carry them across.

[*Continue on rue Saint-Honoré to rue de l'Échelle. Look south to the Louvre.*]

STOP 13 ✻ SITE OF RUE SAINT-NIÇAISE

Métro: Palais-Royal/Musée du Louvre

THE INTERSECTION WHERE RUE SAINT-NIÇAISE MET PLACE DU CARROUSEL IN FRONT OF THE TUILERIES WAS THE SITE OF A FAMOUS ATTEMPT TO ASSASSINATE NAPOLEON. ON December 24, 1800, Josephine, Hortense, and Napoleon's sister Caroline were in the Tuileries preparing to hear Haydn's *Creation* at the Opera. Urged by Josephine to join them, Napoleon set off in the first carriage, driven by his coachman, Caesar. As they pulled out of the Carrousel onto rue Saint-Niçaise, the mounted escort preceding Napoleon's carriage saw an abandoned wagon, on which a large barrel had been tied, partially blocking the road. The escort stopped and ordered the wagon dragged to one side. Rather than waiting until it was completely moved out of the way, Caesar whipped the horses and urged them forward through the narrow opening. Seconds later, the barrel, full of gunpowder, exploded.

Meanwhile, Josephine, Hortense, and Caroline had been briefly delayed. An aide-de-camp escorting the ladies wrote that Josephine was:

> *Wrapping a magnificent new cashmere shawl from Constantinople around her shoulders when I teased her by saying, "Allow me to observe, Madame, that your shawl is not thrown on with your usual elegance." Mme. Bonaparte stopped and good-humoredly begged me to fold it after the fashion of the Egyptian ladies.*

EXPLOSION IN THE RUE SAINT-NIÇAISE

from Napoleon *by Proctor Patterson Jones (1992: Proctor Jones Publishing Company)*

We then stepped into the carriage. The First Consul's équipage had already reached the middle of Place du Carrousel. We drove after it, but had scarcely entered the Place when we heard the explosion. The (bomb) exploded between the carriages of Napoleon and Josephine... .

Hortense was soaked in blood from cuts on her arms. She later wrote, "We felt a violent shock. The carriage seemed to be blown away. The glass in the window broke and fell on us ... our horses, terrified at the noise, reared and dashed back with us to the Tuileries." Napoleon was safely at the concert before he knew what had happened. Upon learning that Josephine was unhurt, he remarked to the officers in his box, "Well, gentlemen, we have had a narrow escape. The scoundrels!" then returned to reading his program.

The bomb, planted by two Royalists later tried and executed, caused tremendous destruction; twenty people died and sixty-four were wounded. Most of the Tuileries windows were blown out, and forty-six houses and shops were so badly damaged that they had to be torn down.

Continue on rue Saint-Honoré. Pass rue de Marengo, named for another of Napoleon's famous battles. Turn right onto rue de Roule, which becomes rue de la Monnaie. Cross the Seine on the Pont Neuf. Pass Quai de l'Horloge, then turn left onto Quai des Orfèvres, which will become Quai du Marché Neuf, which leads to Notre-Dame.

Jean-Baptiste-Michel Dupreel, after a design by Jean Baptiste Isabey and Pierre Francois Leonard Fontaine:

THE ARRIVAL AT NOTRE DAME, *The Metropolitan Museum of Art, Harris Brisbane Dick Fund, 1930*

STOP 14 ✣ NOTRE-DAME DE PARIS

Métro: Cité

The church's small museum, on rue du Cloître Notre-Dame on the cathedral's north side, has a small display devoted to the Coronation. Included are paintings of the ceremony, as well as several cherubs and golden bees that were part of the original decorations. Open in the afternoon on Wednesdays, Saturdays, and Sundays.

ALL OF FRANCE HAD EXPECTED THAT NAPOLEON WOULD BE CROWNED IN THE CHURCH OF LES INVALIDES, A HOME FOR INJURED AND RETIRED SOLDIERS, BECAUSE OF ITS STRONG association with the military. Napoleon, however, imagined a grander setting–the imposing Gothic cathedral of Notre-Dame. Shabby from years of abuse and neglect during the Revolution, it was completely refurbished for the Coronation by Percier and Fontaine. A triumphal arch and golden statues of Charlemagne and other rulers were erected outside the cathedral and a striking neoclassical set resembling a temple from antiquity was constructed within. Imposing faux-marble columns were added and twenty-four chandeliers with thousands of candles were hung to improve the dim lighting. Elevated platforms with scarlet canopies were built for Napoleon and Josephine's thrones.

As the sun rose, workmen rushed to complete the decorations even as thousands of guests began to arrive. Spectators found their seats and waited in the icy cold while vendors, who had slipped by the ticket-takers,

François Gérard:
EMPRESS JOSEPHINE IN IMPERIAL
COSTUME SEATED ON HER THRONE

François Gérard:
NAPOLEON I IN CORONATION ROBES

peddled sausages, rolls, and bonbons up and down the aisles.

By 11am Napoleon and Josephine's coach had reached the church. They used the adjacent archbishops' palace, torn down in 1831, to dress. While Josephine's makeup was reapplied, her maidservants fastened her train, embroidered with bees, to the shoulders of her white gown. Napoleon's train of crimson velvet, trimmed and lined with ermine, weighed more than eighty pounds. Heralds, pages, chamberlains, priests, cardinals, princes, and princesses lined up as two orchestras struck up a march. Josephine and her attendants, followed by Napoleon and his, slowly walked down the long center aisle. The Pope approached the couple and raised his hand in benediction. Napoleon had deliberately planned that this part of the ceremony be held at the far end of the church, out of view of the many anti-religious former Revolutionists in the congregation.

Several newly commissioned orchestral pieces were performed before the Pope anointed the kneeling couple with holy oil. A silver scepter, sword, orb, ring, and other regalia were brought to the Pope, who carefully blessed each item before handing it to Napoleon. Although there had been hours of heated debate over this, the Pope still thought that he would be placing the crown on Napoleon's head—Napoleon had confided to others that he would decide at the cathedral. The Pope picked up the crown of golden laurel leaves and blessed it. He turned toward Napoleon and, as he did so, Napoleon quickly reached out, seized the crown, and placed it on his own head. The Duchesse d'Abrantès later wrote, "At that moment he really was handsome, and his countenance lit up with an expression no words can convey."

Then Josephine slowly approached the altar, her daughter and sisters-in-law carrying her fifty-foot-long

Jacques-Louis David: CORONATION OF EMPEROR NAPOLEON I AND EMPRESS JOSEPHINE

© *RMN / Art Resource, NY*

crimson train. When she reached the carpeted steps, she knelt at her husband's feet and raised her hands in prayer while she waited for the Emperor to crown her. Napoleon first touched her small gold crown, encrusted with emeralds, to his head, then raised it high in the air and carefully lowered it over her elaborate tiara; lifting it once more, he adjusted her hair and finally set the crown on her head. Josephine arose and returned to her throne. The Bonaparte sisters waited until she had climbed five of the twenty-four steps and then, en masse, dropped her heavy train. Josephine staggered, and the crowd gasped as she nearly fell backwards. Napoleon muttered sharp words to his sisters, who reluctantly picked up the train. Josephine recovered her balance and returned to her seat.

After a lengthy Mass, Napoleon took the constitutional oath promising to "govern only in accordance with the interests, happiness, and glory of the French people." Then the booming voice of a herald echoed through Notre-Dame proclaiming "the most glorious and august Emperor Napoleon–Emperor of the French!" The congregation leaped to its feet, roaring *"Vive l'Empereur!"* The four-hour ceremony ended as three choirs sang, "May the Emperor live for all eternity."

FONTAINEBLEAU

Collection of the author

FONTAINEBLEAU

Fontainebleau is approximately an hour train ride from the Gare de Lyon in Paris. At the Fontainebleau station, take the bus marked "Château" (five miles). The SNCF sells one ticket for both the train and bus. For more information see: www.musee-chateau-fontainebleau.fr

OF NAPOLEON AND JOSEPHINE'S THREE MAJOR OFFICIAL RESIDENCES, FONTAINEBLEAU, A SUMPTUOUS RENAISSANCE CHÂTEAU OLDER THAN VERSAILLES, IS THE ONLY ONE still in existence. It was used as a home by Louis XVI and Marie Antoinette in the mid-1780s and, like most palaces, had been emptied of its treasures during the Revolution. In May 1804, a decree allowed Napoleon, already living at the Tuileries and the summer palace of Saint-Cloud (no longer in existence), to use all of Louis XVI's former residences. Although usually frugal, the new Emperor spared no expense to return Fontainebleau to its pre-Revolutionary grandeur, and this was the first royal home that Napoleon and Josephine completely restored and redecorated. Napoleon also dramatically altered the look of the palace by tearing down a western wing to open the front courtyard so he could easily review his troops.

At the peak of the hunting season, the château sometimes housed more than a thousand courtiers, guests, and foreign dignitaries. Scholarly lectures were given in the morning, concerts in the evening and, twice a week, tragedies were staged. Napoleon's sisters, Caroline and Pauline, frequently hosted dances in the ornate ball-

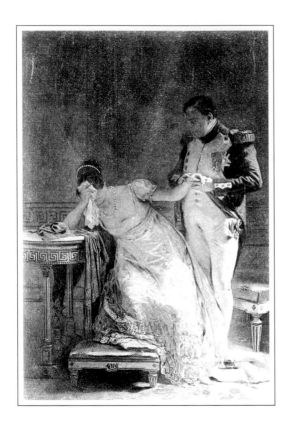

Pagliano:
NAPOLEON ANNOUNCING TO JOSEPHINE
HIS PROJECT OF DIVORCE

New York Public Library Picture Collection

room, but no one could relax and enjoy the festivities. Each time that Napoleon returned from a campaign, the court noticed that he was more short-tempered. By 1807 he insisted that rigid protocol be followed at all times and, whenever he entered a room, the court grew silent, afraid to attract his critical eye. With increasing frustration, Napoleon ordered them to enjoy themselves, commenting, "Strange, I have gathered a good many people here at Fontainebleau. I want them to amuse themselves and have arranged every sort of pleasure, yet everyone has long faces." At the end of one seven-week stay, Josephine received word that her mother in Martinique had died. Instead of allowing the Empress to mourn, Napoleon ordered that the news be kept secret so his scheduled festivities would not be interrupted.

In October 1809, Napoleon renewed an affair with Polish countess Marie Waleska, who became the second of his mistresses to bear him a son. Napoleon now had irrefutable proof he could father a child and was eager to divorce Josephine. He left the army in Germany and arrived at Fontainebleau several days earlier than expected; only an astonished gatekeeper and one staff member were there to welcome him. Predictably, he flew into a rage. When Josephine reached the château that evening and came to greet him, for the first time he did not kiss her, take her hand, or even stand up; he simply looked up from his desk and remarked, "Well, Madame, so you finally arrive. I was about to leave." Josephine then discovered that the doors connecting her private rooms to Napoleon's had been locked. Napoleon continually slighted her in front of the embarrassed guests and courtiers. Hortense later wrote, "The Emperor became unjust…as though he was seeking to make her desire what he did not yet dare to ask for himself, namely a divorce. …His mind was made up, but his heart still

The Forest of Fontainebleau

*D*uring the 1700s and 1800s the vast forest surrounding Fontainebleau was filled with deer and other wild game. Napoleon decided that, just as centuries of Bourbon kings had done, he and Josephine would spend six to eight weeks at the château every fall for the hunting season. The elaborate stag hunts were scheduled three times a week regardless of the weather. Napoleon required that the women wear new, picturesque costumes as they rode in open carriages. The Empress and her ladies wore purplish-pink gowns with a three-cornered black velvet cap topped by snow-white feathers; Hortense and her companions dressed in sapphire blue; Pauline's entourage was in lilac; and Caroline's in cerise. Napoleon also instructed the men to wear new hunting uniforms: bright green coats with gold buttons and lace trim, white cashmere pants, and tall black boots. One of Josephine's staff recalled that, "The brilliant costumes of the court, worn on horseback or in carriages, had a charming effect in the beautiful forest."

resisted. Perhaps he also was trying to prepare my mother."

Soon his family arrived, and Napoleon told them of his decision to remarry. His gloating sisters dropped broad hints to the Empress regarding her impending change in position. For the first time, Napoleon went riding in the late afternoon with his sister Pauline instead of Josephine. Pauline, in return, gave large parties in her suite without inviting Josephine and found a new lover for the Emperor. The resulting affair caused tremendous gossip. Each evening, after saying goodnight to the court, Josephine would retire to her room. From her window, she watched the lights burning in Pauline's apartments in the opposite wing. One of her staff recalled, "God knows how many sleepless nights she spent peering across the shadows of the darkened courtyard."

✦

On November 14, 1809, the couple returned to Paris, where Napoleon finally told Josephine "our divorce has become a political necessity." During an evening ceremony in the Emperor's study at the Tuileries on December 15, the divorce was finalized. Invitations had been sent out to the event as if it were a party. Napoleon's family attended and, as Hortense said, "their joy was apparent." The Empress sat near her children while the Act of Separation was read. Napoleon said Josephine "adorned fourteen years of my life; the memory of that will always remain in my heart." She, in turn, tried to read a brief speech but was unable to continue. Napoleon, followed by Josephine and all the Bonapartes, then signed the separation papers. The next day, wagons stacked high with the Empress's belongings lined up in the Carrousel, and left for Malmaison.

Three months after divorcing Josephine, Napoleon married 19-year-old Austrian archduchess Marie-Louise. In 1811 they had a son, whom Napoleon gave the title "King of Rome." The following year, France's ill-fated invasion of Russia resulted in almost 500,000 dead, and Napoleon became unpopular both at home and across Europe. In 1813, Russia, England, Prussia, and Sweden joined forces to put an end to his constant warfare. On New Year's Day, 1814, Allied forces crossed the French border headed for Paris. Napoleon and his outnumbered army returned to France, arriving at Fontainebleau to discover that Napoleon's brother Joseph had surrendered the city. Although many of his generals deserted, Napoleon's troops were still loyal and he could have continued to fight. But after sleepless nights sequestered in his private apartments, Napoleon made the difficult decision to abdicate in favor of his young son. Shortly thereafter, the French senate decided that the exiled Bourbon family should return to the throne and Napoleon, still at Fontainebleau, was forced to sign another abdication paper for himself and his son. He was to be banished to the tiny island of Elba off the coast of Italy to rule with the absurd title of "Emperor of Elba."

Haunted by the belief that he should not have abdicated, Napoleon contemplated suicide during his last days at Fontainebleau. He had a vial of poison which he carried in a leather pouch around his neck, containing a mixture of belladonna and opium strong enough to kill two men, which his doctor had prepared for him to take if captured by the enemy during the Russian campaign. In his bedroom on April 11, Napoleon swallowed the poison and slipped into unconsciousness; however, the lethal concoction had lost some potency in the eighteen months since it had been prepared and a doctor was able to save his life.

Although Napoleon lived, he was seriously ill and unable to walk for several days. Soon he acknowledged, "one commits suicide to escape disgrace, not misfortune," and started to plan for the voyage to Elba. By April 16, he was well enough to write one last letter to his ex-wife telling her, "My fall is great, but…I shall substitute the pen for the sword (to write) the history of my reign. …Remember him who has never forgotten you and never will. Goodbye, Josephine."

Just before noon on April 20, 1814, Napoleon, still weak, slowly walked down the horseshoe-shaped staircase to the courtyard of the deserted palace, where the last of the Imperial Guard stood waiting. His voice broken by small fits of coughing, he delivered one last impassioned speech to his men. In his memoirs, Chateaubriand described the scene:

The remnants of the soldiers who conquered Europe lined up in the large courtyard, as if on their last battlefield. Napoleon addressed these words to the last witnesses of his battles, "Soldiers of my Old Guard, for twenty years I've always found you on the path of honor and glory. Do not abandon France—love her always, love her well. I bid you farewell, and I kiss your flags."

Napoleon was to return to Fountainebleau once more. He escaped from Elba, landed near Cannes on March 1, 1815, and began marching to Paris with a tiny group of soldiers. The troops sent to arrest Napoleon rallied around him and, by the time Napoleon reached Fontainebleau, Louis XVIII had fled. On March 20, 1815, in his

Horace Vernet and Alphonse-Antoine Montfort: THE FAREWELL OF NAPOLEON I TO THE IMPERIAL
GUARD IN THE COURTYARD OF THE WHITE HORSE AT FONTAINEBLEAU

familiar gray overcoat and black hat, Napoleon stepped out of a dusty carriage into the courtyard. His grenadiers exploded with shouts of *"Vive l'Empereur!"* and joyfully threw their caps in the air. Napoleon held a quick, emotional review of his troops before setting off to Paris and leaving, for the last time, the château he once called "the home of true kings."

MALMAISON

Collection of the author

CHÂTEAU DE MALMAISON

Métro: 1 Line or RER Line A to Grande Arche de la Défense. Transfer in the station to bus #258 (Arrêt-Château), which stops near Malmaison.

ON DECEMBER 16, 1809, THE DAY FOLLOWING HER DIVORCE, JOSEPHINE LEFT PARIS HEADED FOR HER FAVORITE HOME; THE IDYLLIC COUNTRY RETREAT OF MALMAISON JUST west of the city. Napoleon had allowed her to keep the title of Empress and given her a handsome settlement—a huge annual allowance, the Elysée palace on the rue du Faubourg Saint-Honoré, and ownership of Malmaison, where she would maintain a luxurious court.

As soon as Josephine arrived at Malmaison, she began to receive affectionate letters from Napoleon, at first several times daily, then regularly once a week. He visited her frequently during the first six months after the divorce, and the couple strolled through the vast garden or sat on a bench talking as they watched Josephine's Australian black swans swimming in the lake. Josephine opened Malmaison's grounds to the public, and a never-ending stream of guests wandered through her property. Sometimes the Empress herself would appear to give them a tour of the park and point out the cedar of Lebanon tree that she and Napoleon had planted in 1800, which she named "the cedar of Marengo" in honor of Napoleon's great victory in Italy; the tree still stands behind the château. In the years following her divorce, Josephine transformed her oval State Bedroom, still

Life at Malmaison

Nowhere, except on the field of battle, did I ever see Bonaparte happier than in the gardens of Malmaison. - Bourrienne

Before Napoleon sailed for Egypt in 1798, he instructed Josephine to find a country home. Although Malmaison was little more than a glorified farmhouse already more than a hundred years old, Josephine loved it and purchased it in April 1799. Percier and Fontaine began to remodel the château, an early commission in what was to become a long collaboration with Napoleon. They created a tented room with striped walls and trompe l'oeil panels of helmets and swords to be Napoleon's Council Room, as well as a coral dining room with painted panels of dancers. The family spent as much time in the gardens as inside the house. They often piled outside for hours of a lively game called "prisoner's base," frequently played at night while servants held torches. Around this time, Josephine began collecting unusual pets and soon owned a large menagerie with antelopes, kangaroos, zebras, and a favorite orangutan. Malmaison's staff of botanists carefully tended hothouses filled with jasmine, camellias, and several hundred species of flowers never before seen in France. In 1802 a small theatre was added where Hortense, Eugène, and many of Napoleon's relatives and staff acted in productions such as The Barber of Seville. *As many as three hundred guests were regularly invited, and Napoleon himself enthusiastically suggested plays and sometimes acted as stage manager.*

intact today, into a magnificent crimson-tented room; however, she insisted that Napoleon's rooms be kept exactly as he left them and she painstakingly dusted his study herself to ensure nothing would be changed.

After Napoleon left for Elba, Josephine was disconsolate. She was horrified when she learned that Napoleon's young wife had returned to Vienna rather than live with him in exile. She quickly sent Napoleon what would become her last letter to him:

> *Why can I not fly to you? I have been on the point of quitting France to follow in your footsteps. ...Say but the word and I depart. It is no longer by words that my sentiments for you are to be proved, and for actions your consent is necessary. Malmaison has been much respected, and I am surrounded by foreign sovereigns but would rather leave.*

Barely a month after Napoleon left France for Elba, Josephine caught a bad cold. On May 29, 1814, the 50-year-old Empress died in her son Eugène's arms. Her body lay in state at Malmaison for several days as almost 20,000 mourners passed through the columned vestibule, draped in black and lit by hundreds of candles. Napoleon learned of her death months later while reading an out-of-date French periodical. Shocked, he shut himself in his rooms and refused to see anyone but his Grand Marshall for days.

In February of 1815, Napoleon escaped from Elba and returned to Paris to rule for the tumultuous period known as the 100 Days. He asked Hortense, who had not returned to her mother's house since the Empress's

Pierre-Paul Prud'hon:
EMPRESS JOSEPHINE AT MALMAISON

death, to spend the day with him at Malmaison. Early on the morning of April 12, 1815, Napoleon arrived at the château, and he and Hortense walked through the hushed house. Before he left later that day, Napoleon spent hours alone in Josephine's room near the bed in which she died. Josephine's distinctive golden swan bed is still in her room at Malmaison.

Hortense once again opened Malmaison to her stepfather two months later, after his defeat at Waterloo. She wrote, "I felt sad to think how this place, which he visited at the height of his success and fame, now received him reduced to the last stage of wretchedness." Napoleon was at that point considered a fugitive, but lingered at Malmaison surrounded by faithful troops. Finally, as Prussian soldiers neared Malmaison with orders to seize or shoot the former Emperor, Napoleon decided to sail for the United States. Although everything was ready for his departure, early on June 29 his old spirit suddenly resurfaced. He dictated a bold proposition outlining a plan for defeating the Prussians and British and requesting that the new Provisional Government give him temporary command of the army to defend Paris. He closed his letter by saying, "I promise on my word as a citizen and soldier to leave the country the very day I save the capital." In full dress uniform, Napoleon paced the ground-floor salons of Malmaison anxiously awaiting a reply. Hours passed before his aides returned to tell him that the hostile government refused his offer. Napoleon said bitterly, "I wished to make a last effort for France. Now I have nothing to reproach myself with." He changed into civilian clothes and then, just before five in the afternoon, bid a quick farewell to his family before climbing into a carriage headed for the coast of France. He would never see Malmaison or his family again.

Redouté

During the First Empire, several hundred species of flowers never before seen in France were grown at Malmaison. Josephine's collection eventually included more than 250 varieties of roses, and she is credited as having the world's first rose garden. She hired renowned botanists and horticulturalists, and Malmaison's roses are now considered the forerunner of the popular hybrid perennial rose. A rich pink rose with large petals, the Josephinia imperatricis, *also called the* Empress Josephine gallica, *was named for her in 1824 and is still popular today.*

Josephine was proud to be the patron of celebrated artist Pierre-Joseph Redouté (1759-1840), known as the "Raphael of Flowers." His engravings for a three-volume book called Les Roses *became a huge success as did another work,* Jardin de la Malmaison; *Josephine helped fund these projects but died before they were completed.*

JOSEPHINE'S TOMB

CHURCH OF SAINT-PIERRE-SAINT-PAUL 19, BOULEVARD DE GAULLE, RUEIL

The church of Saint Pierre and Saint Paul is a 20-minute walk from Malmaison. Services are held at 8:30am daily and at 6:30pm on Saturday. On Sunday, services are scheduled at 9:30am, 11am, and 6pm. It is recommended to visit during these hours to ensure that the church is open.

When we were at Malmaison, walking the alley leading to Rueil, how many times did the bell of the village church interrupt our most serious conversations? Bonaparte would stop, so the noise of our footsteps would not drown out any portion of the sound that he found so delightful. –Bourrienne

The bells that delighted Napoleon can still be heard around the quaint 16th-century church of Saint Pierre and Saint Paul in Rueil, where Josephine's funeral was held on June 2, 1814. Her tomb lies inside the church to the right of the altar. Following the Empress's death, Hortense and Eugène commissioned a magnificent marble sculpture by the celebrated artist Pierre Cartellier to sit above her tomb. This monument shows the Empress kneeling in the same pose as in Jacques-Louis David's painting *Coronation of Emperor Napoleon I and Empress Josephine* (see p.76).

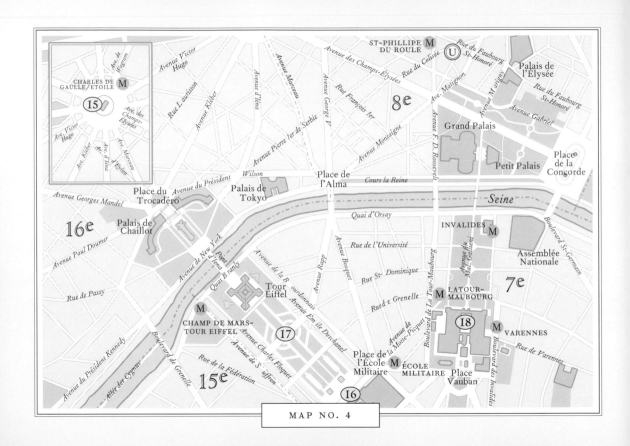

MAP NO. 4

WALK 4

(M) METRO STOP

THE ESCORT AND FUNERAL CHARIOT PASSING UNDER THE ARC DE TRIOMPHE

STOP 15 ✸ ARC DE TRIOMPHE DE L'ÉTOILE

Métro: Charles-de-Gaulle/Étoile

Note: Rather than in chronological order, Walk Four has been laid out for the convenience of the walker, with all Left Bank stops grouped together. To visit these stops in chronological order, begin with Stops 16 and 17, then travel to the Right Bank for Stop 15, then return to the Left Bank for Stops 18 and 19.

AFTER HIS ABDICATION IN 1815, THE BRITISH HELD NAPOLEON PRISONER FOR SIX YEARS ON THE ISLAND OF SAINT HELENA IN THE SOUTH ATLANTIC. HE LIVED THERE WITH A handful of servants and aides until his death in 1821 when his remains were placed in a grave between two willow trees. The grave had no marker because the British would only allow the tomb to be inscribed "General Buonaparte" and the former Emperor's staff refused to allow their leader to be slighted with so modest a title. Over the next twenty years a growing movement in France demanded that the British relinquish his body.

Sire, you will return to your capital,
Without fighting or fury,
Drawn by eight black horses through the Arch Triumphal
Dressed as Emperor. —Victor Hugo

The History of the Arch

*I*n 1806 Napoleon ordered architect Jean-François Chalgrin to build a new monument dedicated to the Grande Armée that was "big, simple, and majestic." The arch was built on the site of one of the old city gates, the Barrière de l'Étoile, the gate of the star, where five roads leading to villages outside Paris converged. Despite his worries that the proposed location was too far from the city, Napoleon accepted a minister's advice that "An arch there would form a majestic view for the Tuileries and could also be seen by visitors entering Paris from a great distance. Additionally, your Majesty would pass through it on his way to Malmaison, Saint-Germain, Saint-Cloud, and Versailles." Construction required more than thirty years and a succession of architects, and Napoleon never saw the arch completed. Napoleon insisted that the monument be built of French stone, from quarries near Fontainebleau, and that it be covered in friezes and sculpture commemorating his military career. The Triumph of Napoleon in 1810 *by Jean-Pierre Cortot can be found on the left side of the arch facing Avenue des Champs-Élysées. The most famous relief, François Rude's* The Departure of the Volunteers (La Marseillaise)*, is on the right side of the arch facing Avenue des Champs-Élysées. Names of battles won by Napoleon are engraved around the arch's top, and 386 generals who served under him are listed on the inside walls; the names of those who died in action are underlined. A small museum inside the arch is devoted to the story of its construction.*

In 1840 Hugo's words became reality when King Louis–Philippe arranged for Napoleon's remains to be brought back from Saint Helena. A stately new tomb was built in the Hôtel des Invalides (see p. 111), and a magnificent funeral procession planned for December of 1840. The grand cortège would make only one stop: at the Arc de Triomphe de l'Étoile, where Napoleon's coffin would briefly rest beneath the giant arch he had commissioned 34 years earlier. The funeral procession would then continue down the Champs-Élysées, through Place de la Concorde, where it would cross the Seine, and end at Les Invalides.

On December 15, 1840, a freezing but sunny day, thousands watched from roofs and windows and gathered near the arch to catch a glimpse of the coffin. Vendors hawked bourbon and cigars to more than 100,000 bystanders who stamped their feet in the cold and peered through rows of glittering bayonets held by the National Guard. Red, white, and blue flags, emblazoned with eagles and the names of Napoleon's battles adorned every corner. Statues depicting his victories had been placed all the way from the arch to Pont de la Concorde. Urns burning incense lined the parade route, and fragrant smoke floated through the chilly air. The entire length of the Champs-Élysées had been sprinkled with sand so that soldiers would not slip on the ice.

The parade assembled early in the morning at Courbevoie, four miles north of Paris. It marched south through the town of Neuilly and finally neared the Arc de Triomphe. Hundreds of mounted soldiers led the procession, followed by generals and veterans of the Grande Armée on foot in the same uniforms they wore while serving Napoleon. The head of the cortège marched to the sound of trumpets and drums, while violinists and a choir of six hundred accompanied the end of the procession, where a grenadier led a lone white

Egyptomania

Paris is filled with references to Egypt dating from Napoleon's military campaign of 1798 and 1799. Until this expedition, Europeans knew very little about Egyptian culture. When Napoleon sailed for Egypt with his troops, he took along more than 160 of France's most famous artists, writers, scientists, and mathematicians so that they could study the ancient civilization. One of the artists was Josephine's good friend, engraver Vivant Denon, after whom a wing of the Louvre is named. When Denon returned, he published a series of drawings in a book called Travels in Upper and Lower Egypt. *The book became a sensation, and Parisians developed a passion for all things Egyptian. Egyptian motifs, such as obelisks and pyramids, were incorporated into architecture. Napoleon commissioned a dinner service of Sèvres porcelain painted with scenes from Egypt; some of the china can be seen at Fontainebleau's Musée Napoleon 1er or at the Louvre. Several other sites in Paris were named for Napoleon's Egyptian campaign, including rue d'Aboukir, Passage du Caire, and rue des Pyramides.*

stallion by the bridle. The horse, draped in purple velvet, wore Napoleon's saddle and was identical to the snow-white steeds the Emperor often rode on the battlefield.

At the end of the procession was the funeral chariot with the coffin. More than 30 feet tall, it was pulled by 16 jet-black horses wearing ivory plumes. Five hundred sailors marched in double file alongside the casket. Parisians watched silently as the grand procession neared the arch. The funeral music stopped and, as the parade began to slow, all that could be heard was the sound of hooves and marching feet crunching along the sanded avenue. The horses drew Napoleon's casket underneath the arch and halted. There was a long moment of eerie silence as frosty rays of sunlight lit the coffin and the stately arch. Spontaneously the crowd erupted with a deafening roar of "*Vive l'Empereur!*" that echoed up and down the Champs-Élysées. Then, in a wave of patriotic euphoria, the National Guard broke into an unrehearsed rendition of *La Marseillaise*, the old Revolutionary anthem loved by Napoleon.

> *Walk back to the Métro at Étoile and take the No. 1 Line (toward Château de Vincennes) three stops to Concorde. Transfer there to the No. 8 Métro (toward Balard) to the École Militaire stop. Walk through place de l'École Militaire and proceed southwest on Avenue de La Motte-Picquet. Avenue de La Motte-Picquet becomes place Joffre at the École Militaire.*

Jacques-Louis David:
NAPOLEON CROSSING THE ALPS

© *RMN / Art Resource, New York*

STOP 16 ❄ ÉCOLE MILITAIRE

IN OCTOBER 1784, FIFTEEN-YEAR-OLD NAPOLEON BONAPARTE ARRIVED AT THE PRESTI-GIOUS ÉCOLE ROYALE MILITAIRE. HE HAD LEFT HIS FAMILY AT AGE NINE TO BEGIN training to become a professional soldier and had already spent several years at the royal military school in Brienne-le-Château. In the 1780s more than 120 cadets, ages thirteen to fifteen, were enrolled in Paris's École Militaire. During Napoleon's time, many who attended were from wealthy, high-ranking families. Napoleon, however, was a charity student. Only boys from families who could prove their nobility for at least four generations were eligible for scholarships, and competition was fierce.

The young cadet was fascinated by ancient Rome and Greece and devoured books about the lives and military tactics of great generals—many of the theories of war and governing he later used were based on his studies of Julius Caesar, Alexander the Great, and Hannibal. He also learned how mathematics and geometry applied to artillery and studied diligently, well aware that the artillery, considered the most difficult military science to learn, offered the best chance for advancement to those not born into prominent noble families.

Napoleon was unpopular with his fellow cadets, whom he openly criticized for indulging in the luxuries provided by the school: five-course dinners with wine and several desserts; servants who cleaned students' uniforms and changed their linen three times a week; and grooms who cared for their horses. Napoleon felt strongly

Napoleon's Bicorne

Napoleon's hat, called a bicorne, is his most enduring and recognizable symbol. Other generals had worn hats in this style, but Napoleon was the first to turn it so it was worn parallel to the shoulders. As First Consul, he usually ordered four each year, but often lost them in battle. Between 1803 and 1815, he most likely wore fifty, several of which may be seen at the Musée de l'Armée, Malmaison, and Le Procope. He usually traveled with a case containing a dozen hats maintained by his longtime valet, Constant. The Emperor's official hatter, Poupard, whose shop was located at 32, Galerie Montpensier in the Palais-Royal, had a large sign outside which read Le Temple de Goût (the "Temple of Taste"). Although Poupard charged exorbitant rates, the felt hats were beautifully constructed, extremely light, lined with gray silk, and decorated with a tricolor rosette. A general who served with Napoleon commented that when Napoleon donned his general's hat, he seemed to grow two feet taller. When angered, Napoleon was known to hurl the hat to the ground and kick it.

that the students would be better soldiers if they learned to perform these tasks themselves, and also proposed that they should eat the simple rations given to the army rather than the school's rich dinners. He was particularly incensed that boys from poor families were introduced to a lifestyle they had little chance of sustaining.

In February 1785, four months after Napoleon arrived in Paris, he received word that his father had died, leaving Napoleon's mother with five young children to support. Distressed about her precarious financial situation, Napoleon decided that he must start earning money to send to his mother. Although it usually took three years to become an artillery officer, he petitioned to take the final examination after only one year. His instructors, hoping to be rid of the opinionated boy, readily agreed. After six months of intense study, Napoleon took the final examination in September 1785. Only four cadets from his school passed, Napoleon among them.

In October 1785, the sixteen-year-old prepared to join a well-respected regiment in Valence where he would perfect his skills. His knowledge of artillery soon became so thorough that he matter-of-factly stated, "If there is no one to make gunpowder for the cannons, I can make it; gun carriages, I know how to construct. If it is necessary to cast cannons, I can cast them; if it is necessary to teach the details of drill, I can do that too." One of Napoleon's favorite expressions as a student was, "God is on the side with the best artillery."

Standing at the École Militaire, turn and face the Eiffel Tower. The Parc du Champ-de-Mars lies between the École Militaire and the Eiffel Tower.

Jacques-Louis David: DISTRIBUTION OF THE IMPERIAL EAGLES TO THE ARMY

STOP 17 ❦ LE CHAMP‑DE‑MARS

FROM THE SEINE TO THE ÉCOLE MILITAIRE
Métro: École Militaire

THE CHAMP-DE-MARS WAS A HUGE TRACT OF LAND USED BY THE SCHOOL AS A PARADE GROUND BEGINNING IN 1770. WHEN NAPOLEON FIRST DRILLED HERE AS A YOUNG CADET in 1784, this area was a sprawling open field much larger than the park seen today. It was Napoleon's favorite parade ground, and for more than fifteen years he held grand military rallies here. The most famous was a lavish ceremony, three days after the Coronation, in which the Emperor presented the army with battle standards bearing his new imperial emblem, a fierce golden eagle. Percier and Fontaine built a majestic temporary stage several stories high, and soldiers were placed in tight formation all the way to the Seine. At the height of the ceremony, Napoleon, wearing his golden crown of laurel leaves and his Coronation robes, rose from his throne and shouted, "Soldiers, behold your standards! These eagles will always serve as your rallying point. Will you swear to defend them with your life?" The men let out a mighty yell to pledge their allegiance.

Walk back to the École Militaire. Walk down Avenue de La Motte-Picquet and turn left at Boulevard de la Tour-Maubourg. At rue Saint-Dominique turn right. Continue to the Esplanade des Invalides. Turn right at Avenue du Mal. Gallieni and head toward the Hôtel des Invalides.

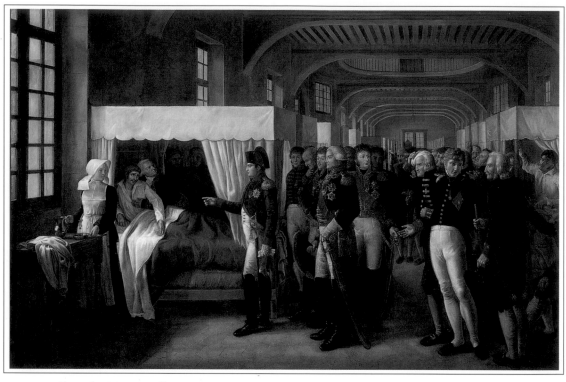

Alexandre Vernon-Bellecourt: NAPOLEON I VISITING THE INFIRMARY OF INVALIDES

© *RMN / Art Resource, New York*

STOP 18 ❊ HÔTEL NATIONAL DES INVALIDES & NAPOLEON'S TOMB

Métro: La Tour-Maubourg

It is my wish that my ashes repose on the banks of the Seine, in the midst of the French people, whom I have loved so well. —Napoleon (in his will, dated April 15, 1821)

NAPOLEON'S REQUEST IS NOW INSCRIBED IN BLACK MARBLE OVER THE ENTRANCE TO THE CRYPT THAT HOLDS HIS REMAINS DEEP INSIDE THE CHURCH OF THE DOME IN LES Invalides. Nineteen years after Napoleon died, Louis—Philippe concluded negotiations with the British for the return of the former Emperor's remains. When the coffin was opened in October of 1840 to identify the body, French and British officials were astounded to see that, although the body had not been embalmed, it had not decayed, but mummified, starting rumors that his death had been caused by poison. Napoleon's body was dressed in his familiar colonel's uniform as a Chasseur of the Guard, his trademark hat across his knees. Coins bearing his image had been laid on the white satin lining of the coffin, and personal items, such as his knife and fork, had been placed inside. Napoleon's heart lay in an urn at his feet; he had requested that it be sent to his wife, Marie-Louise, who refused to accept it.

The remains of the Emperor with his royal escort sailed from Saint Helena and landed at Cherbourg on

November 30. Several of his generals met Napoleon's body at Le Havre, where his remains were placed on a steamboat that traveled up the Seine and arrived in Paris on the morning of December 15. Just before 3pm, the dull roar of cannons announced that Napoleon's coffin was nearing Les Invalides. Thirty-two elaborate, fifteen-foot-tall statues of France's greatest heroes, including Charlemagne, Jeanne d'Arc, and Louis XIV lined the Esplanade. In the center stood a massive plaster statue of Napoleon in his Coronation robes.

More than 40,000 spectators gathered to see Napoleon's casket arrive at its final resting place. When the parade reached the esplanade, the coffin, covered with a huge red cross and bearing Napoleon's crown, was lifted off the enormous horse-drawn hearse and carried on the shoulders of thirty-six sailors. Inside, Louis–Philippe, in a solemn ceremony, accepted Napoleon's remains "in the name of France." He ordered that the sword Napoleon used at Austerlitz and the hat he wore at the battle of Eylau be placed on top of the coffin. Napoleon's casket was temporarily set in the center of the church under the dome, where a quarter of a million people filed past it in the next two days. It was then moved to the chapel of Saint-Jerôme in the Dome Church where it lay until 1861, when Napoleon's permanent tomb was completed. Inside the sarcophagus, Napoleon's body is encased in six coffins, one of zinc, one of mahogany, two of lead, one of ebony, and one of oak.

SHOPS & RESTAURANTS

WALK ONE

(A)
BREGUET • 20 PLACE VENDÔME
www.breguet.com • *Phone: 01 47 03 65 00* • *Métro: Madeleine, Opéra*

Napoleon bought three timepieces from this renowned clockmaker just before he left on his Egyptian campaign: two self-repeating watches and a traveling clock à almanach. Several years later Josephine became a patron and, in 1810, Breguet created the world's first wristwatch for Napoleon's younger sister, Caroline, Queen of Naples. Breguet recently introduced a model entitled *La Reine de Naples* in the style of Caroline's watch. A small museum, open by appointment only, displays historic items including a gold watch of Caroline's.

(B)
CHAUMET • 12 PLACE VENDÔME
www.chaumet.com • *Phone: 01 44 77 24 00* • *Métro: Madeleine, Opéra*

This jeweler's first commission for Napoleon was his ceremonial sword that contained the massive Regent Diamond (now in the Louvre). The firm soon became an official jeweler to the Emperor and Empress and designed many jeweled head ornaments for the Bonapartes, including a famous cameo and pearl tiara for Josephine.

(C)
MELLERIO DITS MELLER • 9 RUE DE LA PAIX
www.mellerio.fr • *Phone: 01 44 55 35 70* • *Métro: Madeleine, Opéra*

Still owned by the same family as during the Empire, this jeweler, the oldest in Paris, created numerous items for Josephine. The shop was originally located on rue Vivienne near the Palais-Royal; in 1815 they moved to their current location.

ANCIENNE MANUFACTURE ROYALE ✦ II RUE ROYALE (*in the Bernadaud boutique*)
www.manufacture-royale.com ✦ *Phone: 01 47 42 61 51* ✦ *Métro: Madeleine, Concorde*

Ancienne Manufacture Royale (Former Royal Manufacturer) became part of the royal Sèvres porcelain workshops, under the protection of King Louis XVI, in 1784. Founded in 1737, one of the company's most popular collections today is their historical cups and saucers series, which features several designs introduced during the Directory, Consulate, and Empire. *Aux Oiseaux* (With Birds), which dates to 1810, was originally manufactured by the Dagoty brothers, official suppliers to Empress Josephine, who owned a successful porcelain factory on the Left Bank. The set consists of a gold trimmed black cup, saucer, and dessert plate. It is decorated with an Egyptian-inspired design showing colorful exotic birds that Josephine, who owned several parrots, adored. An original can be seen at Malmaison.

BOUTIQUE MAILLE ✦ 6 PLACE DE LA MADELEINE
www.maille.com ✦ *Phone: 01 40 15 06 00* ✦ *Métro: Madeleine*

Maille has been selling mustards and vinegars since 1747. The oak-paneled shop still sells fresh mustard from barrels, as was the manner in the 1700s when customers would bring crocks to be filled. At the time of Napoleon's coronation, Maille sold 24 varieties of mustard; *à l'Ancienne*, one of their original blends, has been made from the same recipe for more than 250 years. Maille patrons included Catherine the Great of Russia and Thomas Jefferson, who had Maille's mustards shipped to his Virginia home.

ODIOT ✦ 7 PLACE DE LA MADELEINE
Phone: 01 42 65 00 95 ✦ *Métro: Madeleine*

Several patterns and designs created for Napoleon and his family are still made by Odiot, his official silversmith, and sold in sterling or vermeil. One unusual item is the breast cup used by Napoleon's younger sister Pauline Borghese and her guests to drink punch. Because this cup is made from the original mold taken from Pauline's body, it is not considered a reproduction. Its handle is shaped like a butterfly, which was Pauline's emblem. Odiot also still produces the silver sweet box called a drageoir aux maréchaux that Napoleon presented as a gift to generals who had performed well in battle. Founded in 1690, Odiot created Napoleon's scepter and several other items used in the Coronation.

(G)
HERMÈS • 24 RUE DU FAUBOURG SAINT-HONORÉ
www.hermes.com • *Phone: 01 40 17 47 17* • *Métro: Madeleine*

Hermès has recently reissued their Napoleon scarf. Introduced in 1965, it features a pattern of bees, Napoleon's emblem. A large center medallion shows the Emperor and Empress in their coronation coach; while four corner images depict Napoleon in scenes from well-known military paintings. His Coronation and Consular swords, the sabers he carried in Egypt, and his bicorne and uniform are all incorporated into the design.

(H)
LES DRAPEAUX DE FRANCE • 13, 14, AND 34 GALERIE MONTPENSIER
www.drapeaux-de-france.com • *Phone: 01 40 20 00 11* • *Métro: Palais-Royal/Musée du Louvre*

Hand-painted toy soldiers in authentic uniforms of Napoleon, his Imperial Guard, and the Grande-Armée can be purchased in this picturesque store.

(I)
LIBRAIRIE DE L'ÉCHIQUIER • 149-150 GALERIE DE VALOIS
Métro: Palais-Royal/Musée du Louvre

The walls of this shop are lined with framed letters and documents, all for sale, signed by Napoleon and many of his generals.

(J)
LE GRAND VÉFOUR • 17 RUE DE BEAUJOLAIS
email: grand.vefour@wanadoo.fr • *Phone: 01 42 96 56 27* • *Métro: Palais-Royal/Musée du Louvre*

Built before 1796, the restaurant's original name, Café de Chartres, can still be seen on a sign outside. Josephine and Napoleon dined here frequently.

Phone: 01 42 36 67 21 • Métro: Bourse, Palais-Royal/Musée du Louvre

Prelle has been manufacturing hand-woven luxury silks since 1752. Their fabrics have decorated rooms and furniture at the royal residences of Fontainebleau, Versailles, and the Tuileries. Some fabrics designed for use by Napoleon and Josephine can still be purchased.

STOHRER • 51 RUE MONTORGUEIL

Phone: 01 42 33 38 20 • Métro: Les Halles

One of Paris's oldest bakeries, this historic patisserie has been on the rue Montorgueil for over 270 years. Stohrer, who is credited with inventing the *baba au rhum*, was a pastry chef who traveled to France with Polish princess Marie Leczinska when she married King Louis XV. After serving in the kitchens at Versailles, Stohrer opened this store in 1730.

WALK TWO

AU PLAT D'ÉTAIN • 16 RUE GUISARDE
Phone: 01-43-54-32-06 • Métro: Saint-Sulpice

This store, established before the French Revolution, offers beautiful hand-painted lead toy soldiers. Several different sizes and poses of Napoleon and his marshals are available. Showcases display elaborate battle scenes with officers and soldiers, all in authentic costumes.

LIBRAIRIE PINAULT • 27 AND 36 RUE BONAPARTE
email: abbaye-pinault@wanadoo.fr • Phone: 01 46 33 04 24 • Métro: Saint-Germain-des-Prés

This antiquarian bookstore also sells autographed letters written by Napoleon's marshals and the Emperor himself. Purchases considered very rare must be approved by the Ministry of Culture before being allowed to leave France.

ARTHUS BERTRAND • 6 PLACE SAINT-GERMAIN-DES-PRÉS
www.arthus-bertrand.fr • Phone: 01.49.54.72.10 • Métro: Saint-Germain-des-Prés

This two-story shop, founded in 1803, sells authentic Legion of Honor medals, some with diamonds. The prestigious star-shaped award of merit, supposedly designed by Jacques-Louis David, was established by Napoleon to reward excellence in military or civil service. Inside the store is a display showing the evolution of the medal throughout the years.

DEBAUVE & GALLAIS • 30 RUE DES SAINTS-PÈRES
www.debauve-et-gallais.com • Phone: 01 45 48 54 67 • Métro: Saint-Germain-des-Prés

Debauve & Gallais, official chocolate purveyor to Napoleon and the most famous chocolatier of the 1800s, still makes candy using the original recipes. A specialty is milk chocolate with almonds, a combination invented here. The design of the boutique's interior has been attributed to Percier and Fontaine, Napoleon's official architects, and the shop itself is classified a historical monument. The old apothecary jars in the store are a reminder that when Debauve & Gallais began making chocolate, it was considered a medicine used as a painkiller. The store's columns are each adorned with a caduceus, the ancient symbol of medicine; the half-moon-shaped wooden counter is typical of Parisian pharmacies from the 1790s and early 1800s. *There is a branch on the Right Bank at 33 rue Vivienne (Métro: Bourse; Phone: 01 40 39 05 50).*

LE PROCOPE • 13 RUE DE L'ANCIENNE-COMÉDIE
www.procope.com • Phone: 01 40 46 79 00 • Métro: Odéon

One of Bonaparte's favorite haunts as a young officer, Le Procope opened in 1686. Pictures of Napoleon and a letter signed by him hang on the wall; and one of his famous gray hats is prominently displayed near the entrance. Always short of funds during his early years in Paris, Napoleon was known at Le Procope for leaving his hat as security until he paid the bill. Le Procope did not serve meals during Napoleon's day but was popular for its aperitifs, liqueurs, and fruit-flavored sorbets. It claims to be the first place in Paris to serve coffee to the public.

Á LA CIVETTE ✦ 157 RUE SAINT-HONORÉ
Métro: Palais-Royal/Musée du Louvre ✦ Phone: 01 42 96 04 99

This is the oldest cigar store in Paris. Originally located in the arcades of the Palais-Royal, À la Civette has been on this site since the 1700s and is known for its extensive selection.

LA SAMARITAINE ✦ 2 QUAI DU LOUVRE AND 19 RUE DE LA MONNAIE
www.lasamaritaine.com ✦ Phone: 01 04 41 29 29 ✦ Métro: Pont Neuf/La Monnaie

This popular department store has several restaurants with sweeping views of Pont Neuf, Île de la Cité, and Notre-Dame, where the Coronation parade ended. Lunch, tea, and dinner are served at Toupary, a formal restaurant on the fifth floor; there is also an inexpensive rooftop café and a bar. A viewing area offers the same panorama, for a small fee, without having a meal. The store takes its name from a large pump installed near Pont Neuf by King Henri IV in the 1600s. Tourists marveled at this impressive machine, which sat on the Right Bank and delivered water to the Tuileries palace for the fountains. Store hours are available at www.lasamaritaine.com.

GOSSELIN ✦ 125 RUE SAINT-HONORÉ
Closed Mondays ✦ Phone: 01 45 08 03 59 ✦ Métro: Louvre/Rivoli

This bakery's specialty is bread *à l'ancienne*, made as it was in the late 1700s. The recipe requires that the dough sit for two days before adding yeast.

DALLOYAU · 101 RUE DU FAUBOURG SAINT-HONORÉ

www.dalloyau.fr · *Phone: 01 43 59 18 10* · *Métro: Saint-Philippe-du-Roule*

For more than two hundred years the patisserie Dalloyau has thrived in the same building on a street named for the patron saint of bakers and pastry chefs. The shop opened in 1802, before Napoleon became Emperor. Dalloyau also offers a large menu of takeaway entrées and salads; there is a tearoom upstairs. There are several other branches around Paris.

NAPOLEON AND THE LOUVRE

ALTHOUGH THE STAIRCASE SHOWN IN THE PAINTING AT LEFT WAS DEMOLISHED IN THE 1850S, THE COLORFUL COLUMNS OF ONE LANDING STILL EXIST TODAY IN THE SALLE Percier et Fontaine, located in the Denon wing near the famous statue *The Winged Victory of Samothrace*. The nearby Salon Carré was used as a chapel for the wedding of Napoleon and his second wife, Marie-Louise, in 1810; their elaborate nuptial cortège slowly passed through the adjacent Grande Galerie, now used to display Italian paintings.

On August 10, 1793, the Musée Central des Arts, as it was then called, opened in the eastern portion of the Louvre. Formed from King Louis XVI's art collection and from works seized during the Revolution, it marked the introduction of fine art to the French middle and lower classes. From 1796 to 1813, as the French army invaded most of Europe, Napoleon sent the greatest art treasures of each conquered country to France. Over 500 masterpieces were removed from Italy alone. Vivant Denon, whom Napoleon named Director of Museums in 1802, decided which pieces should be kept at the Louvre and which would be sent to other French museums. At this time, seizing artistic treasures was a common practice considered a legitimate part of the victor's spoils. After Napoleon's fall from power, many of these works were returned to their native countries.

In 1803 the museum was renamed Musée Napoléon in honor of the First Consul who, along with Josephine, regularly visited the exhibits and the Salon, a show of new paintings. Napoleon ordered the museum to have days of free admission so that all Parisians could enjoy the art and antiquities. Many rooms from the Musée Napoléon can still be seen in the modern Louvre, including the Rotonde de Mars, Salle des Saisons, and Salle de Diane (all on the ground floor/Denon wing), and the Galerie d'Apollon.

Listed below are some of the works in the Louvre relating to Napoleon. Check with the information desk to confirm locations.

SULLY WING/2ND FLOOR/SALLE A/ROOM 4/PEINTURES
* Unfinished portrait *General Bonaparte* by Jacques-Louis David (see p.10).

SULLY WING/2ND FLOOR/SALLE 56/PRUD'HON
* *Les Noces d'Hercule et de hébé, (The Wedding celebration of Hercules and Hebe)* by Pierre-Paul Prud'hon, an allegorical work done to celebrate Napoleon's second marriage.
* *Le baron Vivant Denon* by Pierre-Paul Prud'hon, a portrait of Napoleon's Director of Museums.
* *Le Roi de Rome* by Pierre-Paul Prud'hon, a portrait of Napoleon and Marie-Louise's son.

SULLY WING/2ND FLOOR/SALLE 54
* *Bonaparte au pont d'Arcole* by Antoine-Jean Gros. This painting depicts a famous incident in which Napoleon, in order to get his troops across a bridge during deadly enemy fire, grabbed a flag and marched alone to the middle of the pont. Here he is seen looking back to see if his soldiers have followed him. Napoleon sat for this painting in 1796. He fidgeted so badly that Josephine wrapped her arms around her husband and made him sit on her lap, so Gros could finish the details of the General's face.
* *La bataille des Pyramides* by François-André Vincent.

SULLY WING/2ND FLOOR/SALLE 61/PEINTURES FRANÇAISES
* *Le maréchal Ney à la redoute de Kovno* by Denis-Auguste-Marie Raffet. Napoleon called Marshal Ney, one of his most famous generals, "the bravest of the brave."
* *Grenadier de la Garde* by Nicolas Toussaint Charlet.

• *Coronation of Emperor Napoleon I and Empress Josephine* by Jacques-Louis David (see p.76). David painted many of these portraits from life; he attended the ceremony in Notre-Dame. He painted himself, sketchpad in hand, in the enormous work; he can be seen in an upper gallery above and to the left of Josephine, exactly where he had been seated.

• *Empress Josephine at Malmaison* by Pierre-Paul Prud'hon (see p.92). Josephine posed many times for this portrait, which she adored, saying, "It is more the work of a friend than a painter." It sat on an easel in her picture gallery at Malmaison until her death, and later hung in her grandson Napoleon III's apartments in the Palais des Tuileries. When he fell from power in 1870, the French government seized the painting and gave it to the Louvre.

• *Pope Pius VII* by Jacques-Louis David. Portrait of the pope who presided at the Coronation.

• *Juliette Récamier* by Jacques-Louis David. This society beauty, a contemporary of Josephine's, was exiled by Napoleon for conspiring with his enemies.

• *Bonaparte visitant les pestiférés à Jaffa (Napoleon in the Pesthouse at Jaffa)* by Antoine-Jean Gros. Napoleon visits some of his soldiers who had contracted the deadly disease during the Egyptian campaign.

• *Napoleon sur le champ de Bataille d'Eylau* (Napoleon at the Battle of Eylau) by Antoine-Jean Gros.

• *Portrait de Murat, roi de Naples* by Baron Antoine-Jean Gros. Napoleon's brother-in-law as king of Naples.

• *Bonaparte franchissant les Alpes* by Paul Delaroche. Napoleon crossed the Alps on a mule as shown here. David's famous painting of the same subject (at Malmaison, see p. 104) takes historical liberties by placing Bonaparte on a rearing horse.

• *The Coronation of Marie de Medicis* by Peter Paul Rubens. David was inspired by the composition of this painting while working on *Coronation of Emperor Napoleon I and Empress Josephine*, Josephine's pose and the positioning of the ladies bearing her train is borrowed from this work.

The Department of Decorative Arts displays many pieces of furniture, china, jewelry, and other objets d'art commissioned by Napoleon and Josephine.

The Galerie d'Apollon exhibits some of the French crown jewels, including the 140-carat diamant le Régent (Regent diamond), which Napoleon first wore mounted in the hilt of his Consular sword and later in his Imperial sword. The Gallery of Apollo is closed for several years; some of its treasures have been moved to the Sully wing/1st floor/Room 64. Other jewels displayed include:

• *A large rose diamond belonging to Queen Hortense, Josephine's daughter*
• *Snuffbox with miniatures of Napoleon and Josephine*
• *Josephine's pearl and diamond earrings*
• *A pair of ruby bracelets, part of a larger set that belonged to Marie-Louise*
• *Hortense's sapphire and diamond parure of necklace, rings, brooch, and tiara*

• Napoleon's tea service by Biennais; a mosaic parure which belonged to Marie-Louise; pieces from Napoleon's famous Egyptian dinner service of Sèvres china; wooden and gilt-bronze washbasin by Biennais which Napoleon took to Saint-Helena.

RICHELIEU WING / 1ST FLOOR / SALLE 71
- Vases and other Sèvres china used by Napoleon in the Tuileries

RICHELIEU WING / 1ST FLOOR / SALLE 72
- Vases and furniture commissioned for Josephine's use in the Tuileries
- Vases, tapestry, and center medallion from Napoleon's throne room in the Tuileries

RICHELIEU WING / 1ST FLOOR / SALLE 73
- The Empress's jewel box, designed by Charles Percier. Commissioned in 1806 for Josephine's bedroom in the Tuileries, this "great casket" was not delivered until after the divorce in 1809 and was subsequently used by Marie-Louise.
- *L'empereur Napoléon 1er en costume de Sacre* by François Gerard.

RICHELIEU / BASEMENT / SCULPTURES FRANÇAISES / SALLE 31
- *Napoleon in Coronation Robes* by Claude Ramey.

The museum's History of the Louvre (*Histoire du Louvre*) section holds Bartolini's massive bronze bust of Napoleon, which originally sat in the entryway of the Musée Napoléon.

NAPOLÉON 1er MUSEUM AT FONTAINEBLEAU

The Musée Napoléon 1er focuses on Napoleon's life as Emperor and houses many rare paintings, memorabilia, and objets d'art. The museum currently has no English guidebook and tours are usually only conducted in French; this brief listing provides highlights of each room.

ROOM I ⋅ Paintings and busts of the Bonapartes, including portraits of Napoleon's mother, Hortense with her son, and Napoleon's siblings and their spouses.

ROOM 2 ⋅ Coronation memorabilia, including Napoleon's Coronation sword and pieces of his costume; Coronation portraits of Napoleon and Josephine; a small snuffbox containing a golden leaf from the crown that Napoleon wore during the ceremony.

ROOM 3 ⋅ China from the Emperor and Empress's personal table services (including pieces from the famous Egyptian dinner service Napoleon commissioned) as well as service pieces from Biennais; Casanova's painting *The Marriage Banquet of Napoleon and Marie-Louise* (some of the actual vermeil serving pieces shown in the painting are displayed).

ROOM 4 ⋅ Gaming tables and portraits of Napoleon's brothers when they were kings.

ROOM 5 • One of Napoleon's military tents with his iron bed, folding chairs, and collapsible wooden table inside; his traveling toiletry case by Biennais; clothing worn by Napoleon, including a bicorne.

ROOM 6 • Uniform worn by Napoleon as a colonel of the Foot Grenadiers of the Imperial Guard (the only known remaining one of its type), his swords, saber, rifles, pistols, and one of his Legion of Honor medals.

ROOM 7 • Menjaud's portrait of Marie-Louise painting Napoleon; the Empress's sewing kit and other personal items.

ROOM 8 • Items relating to Napoleon and Marie-Louise's son, the King of Rome, including the elm and bronze crib used in the nursery at the Tuileries.

ROOM 9 • Toys belonging to the King of Rome, including his drum, miniature cannon, and dominoes; a table decorated with a map of the world acquired by Napoleon in 1810.

ROOM 10 • Layette of the King of Rome.

VERSAILLES

MAIN CHÂTEAU

Although Napoleon never lived in the Main Château, which he called "ugly," his career is featured in two rooms at the end of the Grand Apartments: the Salle du Sacre (Coronation Room), which contains Jacques-Louis David's *Distribution of the Imperial Eagles to the Army* (see p.108), as well as David's own copy of *Coronation of Emperor Napoleon I and Empress Josephine* and the Salle des Marchands (also known as the "1792 Room"), devoted to heroes of the Revolution and First Empire, where a painting of Josephine's first husband, Alexandre de Beauharnais, is also displayed.

The château is home to the Musée Historique du Château de Versailles (Museum of French History), whose Consulate and Empire collection consists of 31 rooms of paintings portraying Napoleon and his family. Both this museum, and the Galerie des Batailles (Gallery of Battles), which displays several monumental battlefield paintings of Napoleon's greatest victories including Austerlitz, Wagram, Rivoli, and Friedland, were assembled by Louis-Philippe in 1837; they are open to the public intermittently.

GRAND TRIANON

Napoleon liked the Grand Trianon, a small classically designed palace on the grounds of Versailles, and sometimes lived there following his divorce from Josephine. Most of the furniture dates to the First Empire, and Napoleon's private apartments, while not as intimate as those at Fontainebleau, can be toured. The Empress's bedroom contains many furnishings used by Marie-Louise, and its imposing bed was created for Napoleon's use at the Tuileries. Napoleon enjoyed working and eating on the columned peristyle and, in 1810, installed large glass panes so that the wind would not disturb him. The panes stayed in place until just before World War I.

PETIT TRIANON

Napoleon allowed his favorite sister, Pauline, to live in this intimate château, beloved by Marie Antoinette.

THE COACH MUSEUM

Usually only open in summer, the museum contains several ornate state carriages used during Napoleon's wedding procession through Paris in April 1810.

Visitors can view the Grand Apartments, the Grand Trianon, and the Petit Trianon in independent visits. Guided tours of other parts of the main château are announced daily when the château opens; it is possible to call that morning (33 1 30 83 77 89) to see which tours are being offered. A calendar of events and more information can be found at: www.chateauversailles.fr.

OTHER PLACES TO VISIT

RIGHT BANK

MUSÉE CARNAVALET
23 rue de Sévigné ◆ Métro: Saint-Paul

Several rooms are devoted to the Consulate and Empire with memorabilia including a copy of the proclamation Napoleon issued after his coup d'état in 1799.

FONTAINE DE LA VICTOIRE
Place du Châtelet ◆ Métro: Châtelet

In 1807 Napoleon commissioned this large fountain, also known as Fontaine du Palmier (palm tree fountain), and column which lists the names of some of his greatest victories.

PETIT HÔTEL BOURRIENNE
58 rue d'Hauteville ◆ Métro: Bonne-Nouvelle
Open on weekend afternoons for tours with appointment only; call 01-47-70-51-14.

This home, with its original Directoire décor intact, was purchased by Napoleon's secretary Louis de Bourrienne in 1801; prior to that, the beautiful Merveilleuse Fortunée Hamelin lived here and often entertained her close friends Mme de Beauharnais (Josephine) and Thérese Tallien in the ground-floor salon.

THÉÂTRE DES VARIÉTÉS
7 boulevard Montmartre ◆ Métro: Rue Montmartre

The Variétés, one of the few theatres from the First Empire still in existence, has been on this site since 1807 and exemplifies the intimate performance rooms that Josephine loved.

PASSAGE DES PANORAMAS
11 boulevard Montmartre ◆ Métro: Rue Montmartre

Joséphine's stationery supplier and Napoleon's official perfumerie were housed in this enclosed shopping arcade, opened in 1799.

PALAIS DE LA BOURSE
Place de la Bourse ◆ Métro: Bourse

Construction of the columned Bourse, home of the French stock exchange, began in 1808, four years after Napoleon was crowned; its neoclassical style typifies much of the architecture of the First Empire.

BANQUE DE FRANCE
31 rue Croix-des-Petits-Champs ◆ Métro: Palais-Royal/Musée du Louvre

Napoleon, as First Consul, founded the Banque de France in January 1800; eight years later, the bank moved into this stately building near the Palais-Royal.

HÔTEL DE TALLEYRAND
2 rue Saint-Florentin and 258 rue de Rivoli ◆ Métro: Concorde

From 1812 to 1838, this was the residence of Charles-Maurice de Talleyrand-Périgord, one of Napoleon's most important ministers, of whom Victor Hugo wrote, "In this palace, like a spider in his web, Talleyrand allured and caught one by one, heroes, thinkers, great men, conquerors, kings, princes, emperors, Bonaparte, Alexander of Russia, Louis XVIII; all the gilded and glittering flies who buzz through the history of the last forty years. This glistening throng, fascinated by the penetrating eye of this man, all passed through the gloomy entrance of 'Hotel Talleyrand.'"

22-24 RUE DES CAPUCINES
Métro: Madeleine

After his successful handling of the royalist insurrection in October 1795, Napoleon was given elegant living quarters here; this was his residence during his romance with Josephine and until their marriage in March of 1796.

LA MADELEINE
Place de la Madeleine • Métro: Madeleine

In 1806, Napoleon ordered that this "Temple of Glory" be dedicated to honor his soldiers; originally started as a church, the long rectangular landmark, with 52 Corinthian columns spanning the exterior, features a mural inside that depicts, among others, Napoleon in imperial robes with a tablet marked "Concordat 1802."

HÔTEL BORGHESE/BRITISH AMBASSADOR'S RESIDENCE
39 rue du Faubourg Saint-Honoré • Métro: Madeleine

Napoleon's younger sister, Princess Pauline Borghese, bought this luxurious home in 1803 and sold it to the British government in 1814; the house still retains much of its Empire décor and furniture and has one of the largest private gardens in Paris.

PALAIS DE L'ÉLYSÉE
55 rue du Faubourg Saint-Honoré • Métro: Champs-Élysées/Clemenceau

Napoleon gave this mansion, previously owned by his sister Caroline and her husband Joachim Murat, to Josephine after their divorce in 1809, although she rarely used it. The Emperor himself lived here for brief periods in 1809, 1812, 1813, and during the "Hundred Days" when crowds gathered on Avenue de Marigny to watch him walking in the garden behind the palace. Napoleon signed his second abdication at the Élysée after the battle of Waterloo in June 1815; it is now the residence of the President of France.

CIMETIÈRE DU PÈRE-LACHAISE
boulevard de Ménilmontant • Métro: Père-Lachaise

The Père-Lachaise Cemetery, opened in 1804, is the final resting place of many of the Empire's marshals and generals, including Joachim Murat and Michel Ney; Napoleon's son, Alexandre Walewska, and the boy's mother, Marie Walewska, Napoleon's favorite mistress, are also buried here.

BAGATELLE CHÂTEAU
Bois de Boulogne, southwest of the Jardin d'Acclimatation • Métro: Les Sablons

The only time Josephine saw Napoleon's son, the "King of Rome" (1811-1832), was at this lovely pavilion, built in 1775 by the Comte d'Artois; Napoleon arranged for the baby to be brought here by a governess while Josephine, who had begged to see the child, waited inside.

LEFT BANK

HÔTEL DES MONNAIES/LE MUSÉE DE LA MONNAIE
11 Quai de Conti • Métro: Pont Neuf/La Monnaie

This museum, which housed the mint during the First Empire, displays coins honoring Napoleon.

10 RUE DE LA HUCHETTE
Métro: St.-Michel

Napoleon was a lodger here, then a cheap furnished hotel called the Blue Dial, when he suppressed the Royalist uprising in 1795.

HÔTEL DE SALM/PALAIS DE LA LÉGION D'HONNEUR
64 rue de Lille • Métro: Musée d'Orsay

In 1804 Napoleon designated this small palace, now home of the museum of the Légion d'Honneur, as the headquarters of the award.

PALAIS BOURBON (NATIONAL ASSEMBLY)
Quai Anatole-France • Métro: Assemblée-Nationale

In 1807 Napoleon added the façade facing the Seine, with its Corinthian columns, so that the building would mirror the classical design of the Madeleine across the river.

HÔTEL DE BEAUHARNAIS/GERMAN AMBASSADOR'S RESIDENCE
78 rue de Lille • Métro: Assemblée-Nationale

Eugène de Beauharnais, Josephine's son whom Napoleon adopted, bought this mansion in 1803 and sold it to the Prussians in 1814. The outside is decorated with a striking neo-Egyptian portico that Eugène, who participated in Napoleon's Egyptian campaign, added in 1804.

PROTESTANT CHURCH OF PENTÉMONT
104-106 rue de Grenelle and l'Abbaye de Pentémont, No.37 rue de Bellechasse, around the corner from 104 • Métro: Solférino

These two buildings were part of the old convent of Notre Dame Pentémont, where 20-year-old Mme de Beauharnais lived from 1783 until 1785 during her separation from her first husband, Alexandre; No. 104-106 rue de Grenelle was used as a chapel, while the building on rue de Bellechasse held the convent, which also served as a boarding house for aristocratic ladies.

CHURCH OF SAINT-GERMAIN-DES-PRÉS
Place Saint-Germain-des-Prés • Métro: Saint-Germain-des-Prés

In October of 1784, fifteen-year-old Napoleone, accompanied by three classmates from the military school of Brienne and a chaperone, arrived in Paris for the first time and knelt in prayer at this church, one of the oldest in the city, before entering the *École Royale Militaire*.

FONTAINE DU FELLAH
Across from 97 rue de Sèvres and just outside the Vaneau Métro station near the Laennes Hospital • Métro: Vaneau

In 1806 Napoleon commissioned this fountain, with its striking statue of a tall Egyptian water carrier; *fellah* is the Arabic word for peasant or farmer.

FONTAINE DE MARS
129-131 rue Saint-Dominique (on the corner of rue Saint-Dominique and rue de l'Exposition) • Métro: École Militaire

In 1806 Napoleon commissioned architect Nicolas Bralle to design this austere neoclassical four-sided fountain. On the side facing the street is a large relief of Hygeia, the goddess of health, gazing at Mars, the god of war, who is wearing an ornate helmet.

Napoleon commissioned several bridges to be built across the Seine; among them are the Pont des Arts, a metal footbridge by the Louvre, Pont d'Austerlitz, and Pont d'Iéna, named after two of his most famous victories.

NOTES

NOTES

NOTES

NOTES

ACKNOWLEDGMENTS

The author wishes to thank Angela Hederman and Nadia Aguiar at The Little Bookroom. The author is grateful for the contributions of: Deborah Esposito, Rachel Fox, Philippe Generali, David Bell, Gilliam Greyson, Jeremie Benoit/Château de Versailles, Guillaume Verzier, Beatrice Grima, Marie-Claude Chira, Olessia Voltchenkova/Prelle, Judith and Andrew Economos, Todd Simon, Sharon Zisman, Nicolas de La Morinière/Odiot, Breguet, Mimi Crume/Hermès, Abigail Caumartin/Bernadaud-Royale, Edwige Gilbert, Diana T. Hodgson, Nancy and Larry Price, Doris and Martin Haig, Will Jennings, Jo Pettet, Ben Newick/British Ambassador's Residence-Paris, Candice Nancel/US Embassy-Paris, Alison Mazer, Eric Splaver, Debauve & Gallais, Chaumet, Ronald Freyberger, Marshall Chapman, Joel Hellman, Gail Ginser, Bob Doyle, Monsy Cruz, Bill Kallam, Danielle Freeman, the Watson Library/Metropolitan Museum of Art, Reidsville Public Library, Rockingham County Public Library, and the New York Public Library.

ABOUT THE AUTHOR

A graduate of Sarah Lawrence College, Diana Reid Haig is an award-winning songwriter, annotator, and audio producer. Her credits include many successful reissues of popular American music, including an Elmore James boxed set that won the W.C. Handy award for "Best Historical Collection." She has produced, annotated, or engineered almost 100 compilations, DVD-As or SACDs for Motown, NBC, Universal, SONY, Warner Bros., and other entertainment companies. A member of the Napoleonic Society of America, her lifelong interest in Paris during the First Empire led her to research and write "Walks through Napoleon and Josephine's Paris," her first book. She lives in New York City and Reidsville, North Carolina with her husband.